# 16 Weeks to COLLEGE SUCCESS

## The Mindful Student

*fourth edition*

Gina Burkart, Ed.D.

Kendall Hunt
publishing company

Figures and tables throughout the text created by Gina Burkart.

Cover images and chapter openers © Shutterstock.com

Kendall Hunt
publishing company

www.kendallhunt.com
*Send all inquiries to:*
4050 Westmark Drive
Dubuque, IA 52004-1840



Pak ISBN: 979-8-7657-8552-2
Text ISBN: 979-8-7657-8553-9



Published in the United States of America

# Contents

# Introduction

Welcome to college! If this is your first semester, you are likely filled with mixed emotions—anticipation, fear of the unknown, excitement and hope for your future, a feeling of independence, and accomplishment. And yet within all of that mix is often an unspoken question that students aren't sure how to ask or who to ask: So, now that I am here, how do I do this? This book will be your answer to that question!

Some of you may not be new to college. This might not be your first semester. You may already have had a semester or two of experience. You might have transferred or had an unsuccessful or unpleasant beginning to college, but you are giving it another try—a fresh start. You might also still be wondering about that unspoken question: How do I do this—college? But, you are also still a little unsure who to ask. This book is also for you. It will answer your question also.

# Week One

# Motivation, Metacognition and Mapping Goals for the Semester

Each successful semester in college begins in the same way that any successful adventure or journey begins—with a plan and goals. As you begin the first week of your semester, your professors will give you a syllabus for the course. The syllabus is your map to your class. It is one of the (if not THE) most important documents of the semester. It is a contract between you and the professor and contains all of the rules, guidelines, assignments, and important dates for your course. Successful students immediately three-hole punch the syllabus and put it in the front of their course binder. Successful students also read the syllabus meticulously, mark, and underline important statements, rules, and dates that the professor emphasizes in class. The syllabus is NOT a document to bury in a folder or to lose. It should be looked at before each class period.

## Activity One

Read through each syllabus you received this week. Underline and highlight important points in the syllabus. The following questions might help you to look for important information. Note anything in the syllabus that is unclear and clarify it with the professor in class or through email.

### Contacting the Professor

Where is the professor's office? How and when can you contact the professor with questions?

### Course Content

What is the purpose of the class?

What types of assignments will you have? When are they due?

## Class Policies

What is the attendance policy?

How many classes can you miss? What is the consequence?

What should you do if you need to miss class or have a family or health emergency?

How will you be graded in the class?

What should you do if you need accommodations?

What is the policy for late work?

Are electronic devices allowed in the classroom?

## Resources

What resources are available to support you with the course?

# Activity Two

Use the syllabus to create a learning plan for each course. See Figure 1.1 for a student sample. You could use the blank templates included to write in your course information for each course—or you could use Smart Art in Word to create your own electronic template similar to Figure 1.1 and print it out and place it in your course binder. If you choose to write in the blank templates in this book, you could photocopy the template and place it in your course binder. Either option would work; the key to success this week is to create a learning plan that contains all the key elements of the course in one place so that you can refer back to it and stay on track throughout the semester.

## Learning Plan

Creating a Learning Plan for each of your courses can help you find control, organization, and success in your learning when everything seems to be chaotic and out of control. Here is a sample learning plan and a template for you to use to keep track of what is going on in your classes and what you will do to find success with these new changes.

This template can also be used at the beginning of every semester to get yourself organized and off to a great start! Good luck! You've got this.

## Figure 1.1: Student Learning Plan Sample

**Course: Philosophy**

**Office Hours/Contact/Technology:**

1. Moodle/Teams
2. Teams Online Meeting chat and video meeting calls/MWF 1–4 pm/Email as needed
3. Text message—phone number

**Note-Taking and Lectures:**

1. Videos will be posted online at the time of class. Videos will also be recorded for students to access in case streaming/Internet fails.
2. Students need to take photos of notes and upload to Moodle for participation points
3. Use Cornell notes for note-taking strategy
4. Summarize and synthesize notes with book notes after class as a study strategy

**Tests and Quizzes:**

1. 1 test every two weeks on Moodle/Fridays at 10 am—100 points/open note and book
2. Weekly quizzes over online lectures—15 points each

**Study Plan:**

1. Synthesize notes with concept maps
2. Read through professor's comments on Moodle
3. Create Concept Cards over key terms and quiz myself
4. Use Bloom's Taxonomy to anticipate exam questions and prepare responses

**Reading Assignments and Reading Plan:**

1. Textbook chapters to be read before viewing class lectures/on Moodle.
2. Book *Sophie's World*—Moodle discussion is related to this book. Assigned readings on Moodle each week.
3. Use careful annotations while reading to prepare for Moodle discussions and essay portions of the test. Marked up text can be used for the test.

**Daily Assignments:**

1. Class readings/See Moodle
2. Moodle discussions
3. Viewing lectures online/note-taking/studying

**Projects/Papers:**

1. Research paper due last week of the semester

**Resources:**

1. Marc—Academic Coaches available in portal/marc.clarke.edu
2. Video call meetings with Gina every Wed for strategies for studying and time management.
3. Writing Center video call meetings with Aimee.
4. Library chats for support with research for final paper.
5. Campus ministry online prayer @ 1 pm for stress relief and wellbeing.

## Figure 1.1: Student Learning Plan

**Course:**

**Office Hours/Contact/Technology:**

1.
2.
3.

**Note-Taking and Lectures:**

1.
2.

**Tests and Quizzes:**

1.
2.
3.

**Study Plan:**

1.
2.
3.

**Reading Assignments and Reading Plan:**

1.
2.

**Daily Assignments:**

1.
2.
3.
4.

**Resources:**

1.
2.
3.
4.

## Figure 1.1: Student Learning Plan

**Course:**

**Office Hours/Contact/Technology:**

1.
2.
3.

**Note-Taking and Lectures:**

1.
2.

**Tests and Quizzes:**

1.
2.
3.

**Study Plan:**

1.
2.
3.

**Reading Assignments and Reading Plan:**

1.
2.

**Daily Assignments:**

1.
2.
3.
4.

**Resources:**

1.
2.
3.
4.

## Figure 1.1: Student Learning Plan

**Course:**

**Office Hours/Contact/Technology:**

1.
2.
3.

**Note-Taking and Lectures:**

1.
2.

**Tests and Quizzes:**

1.
2.
3.

**Study Plan:**

1.
2.
3.

**Reading Assignments and Reading Plan:**

1.
2.

**Daily Assignments:**

1.
2.
3.
4.

**Resources:**

1.
2.
3.
4.

## Figure 1.1: Student Learning Plan

**Course:**

**Office Hours/Contact/Technology:**

1.
2.
3.

**Note-Taking and Lectures:**

1.
2.

**Tests and Quizzes:**

1.
2.
3.

**Study Plan:**

1.
2.
3.

**Reading Assignments and Reading Plan:**

1.
2.

**Daily Assignments:**

1.
2.
3.
4.

**Resources:**

1.
2.
3.
4.

## Figure 1.1: Student Learning Plan

**Course:**

**Office Hours/Contact/Technology:**

1.
2.
3.

**Note-Taking and Lectures:**

1.
2.

**Tests and Quizzes:**

1.
2.
3.

**Study Plan:**

1.
2.
3.

**Reading Assignments and Reading Plan:**

1.
2.

**Daily Assignments:**

1.
2.
3.
4.

**Resources:**

1.
2.
3.
4.

## Figure 1.1: Student Learning Plan

**Course:**

**Office Hours/Contact/Technology:**

1.
2.
3.

**Note-Taking and Lectures:**

1.
2.

**Tests and Quizzes:**

1.
2.
3.

**Study Plan:**

1.
2.
3.

**Reading Assignments and Reading Plan:**

1.
2.

**Daily Assignments:**

1.
2.
3.
4.

**Resources:**

1.
2.
3.
4.

## Activity Three: Self-Assessment

For any plan to be successful, one needs to begin by assessing how and what has worked in the past, what hasn't worked very well, and then form goals based on the valuable information that comes out of that assessment. We assess many things and form many goals—but sadly we seldom take the time to assess ourselves and form our own goals. Successful people realize the importance of self-assessment and goal setting. They take that time to reflect, assess, and set their own goals. Invest in yourself this week. Use the following, self-assessment (Figure 1.2. Self-Assessment) to take the time to reflect on how you have performed in past semesters in the areas that are key to your academic success.

## Figure 1.2: Self-Assessment

**Date:**

(5 is highest)

**1.** How are you feeling about your skills in the following areas:

| | | | | | |
|---|---|---|---|---|---|
| Reading | 1 | 2 | 3 | 4 | 5 |
| Writing | 1 | 2 | 3 | 4 | 5 |
| Note-Taking | 1 | 2 | 3 | 4 | 5 |
| Time Management | 1 | 2 | 3 | 4 | 5 |
| Organization | 1 | 2 | 3 | 4 | 5 |
| Test-Taking | 1 | 2 | 3 | 4 | 5 |
| Oral Communication | 1 | 2 | 3 | 4 | 5 |
| Studying | 1 | 2 | 3 | 4 | 5 |
| Motivation | 1 | 2 | 3 | 4 | 5 |

For those that are not "5," what do you feel would help you get to a "5"?

Which skill areas have most impacted your success in the past?

How can this course help?

**2.** How do you feel about taking this course? Why?

3. What strategies will you use in this course to be successful?

4. What technology needs do you have? How might you address these needs? What gaps may still exist?

5. What challenges do you have this semester that might impact your success in this course that your professor should be aware of? How do you plan to meet these challenges? (Make a plan for communicating needs with professor).

6. What resources will you use to be successful in this course (Ex. Writing Center, Learning Center, Counseling Center, Library, Campus Ministry, IT, Compass/Career Center)?

7. What goals do you wish to make for this semester? What support do you need to achieve these goals?

## Activity Four: Taking the LASSI

The LASSI is a nationally normed self-assessment that helps you see how you compare with other college students in the country on key indicators of college success. This gives you some quantitative data to compare with your own qualitative self-assessment that you completed of yourself in week three. It gives you a chance to integrate additional information into your goals so that you can really see what is impacting your success so that you can focus on it and use the strategies from this text and the support from your college and professor to grow and improve over the course of the semester.

You will take the LASSI again at the end of the semester to see how you have improved and grown.

1. Go to the inside cover of the book if you have a hardcopy of the text and click on the link of the LASSI. For the digital copy of the text, see page following the cover.
2. Read through the results and compare it with your own self-assessment.

## Activity Five: Motivation & Goal Setting

We are motivated when we realize that we need and desire something. Thus, motivation is linked with setting goals and objectives. Not setting realistic goals with specific objectives can negatively impact our motivation and success. Reflecting on our strengths and weaknesses is a great way to begin with goal setting.

Now that you have assessed yourself, it is time to dig a little deeper into the skill areas of academic success and identify your strengths and weaknesses and set specific goals for improving in each skill area. This book also offers specific strategies for improving in each skill area throughout the semester. (*While the book is planned to cover the skills in a logical fashion to help students when they generally need help with the academic skills during the 16-week-semester—students are able to skip ahead and target the specific skill area at any point in the semester as needed. For example, if the self-assessment and goal setting activity revealed that you really need to work on your reading strategies immediately, and this book doesn't cover those until weeks 5 and 6, you may want to look ahead to weeks 5 and 6 and begin working on the reading strategies now.*)

Complete the goal setting questions and chart in Figure 1.3 to identify strengths and weakness in each skill area. As you reflect on each, it is important to begin with your strengths. You may be tempted to skip your strengths and only write down weaknesses. **AVOID this temptation**. It reduces confidence and self-efficacy and sabotages goal setting. In setting goals, you need to **build on your strengths**. To do this, you must first identify them. Everyone has strengths in every area—most of us just don't focus on them. We only focus on our problems and weaknesses. This creates anxiety, fear, and ultimately leads to failure! You want to **SUCCEED**. So begin with your strengths.

As you set goals, be very specific and concrete. Good goals can be measured and assessed. Consider the following example:

> Reading: Strength—comprehension Weakness—takes too long to read; don't read before class

**General Goal: Become a better reader.** *How do you know you are a better reader? How do you measure and verify this goal? How do you demonstrate it and measure it. It is much more difficult to verify. When progress isn't easy to see and measure, goals tend to not be met.*

**More Specific and Measurable Goal: Develop effective and efficient reading strategies that help me to read my textbooks before class.** *This goal could easily be demonstrated. You could show someone at the end of the semester the reading strategies that you were using to efficiently and effectively read your textbook before class. You could also verify whether or not you were doing this.*

## Figure 1.3: Goal Setting

Most Students find success when they make adjustments in the following areas. Use the chart to evaluate yourself in these areas and set some goals. **Example of a specific goal that could be demonstrated and assessed: Time Management: I will create a "to do" list each Sunday and write what I need to get done on my planner for the week.**

**Goal that is too general: Use my time effectively.**

| | | |
|---|---|---|
| **Reading**<br><br>**SMI INFP** | **Strengths:**<br><br>**Weaknesses:** | **Goals** |
| **Organization**<br><br>**MOT ANX TMT ATT** | **Strengths:**<br><br>**Weaknesses:** | **Goals** |
| **Studying**<br><br>**SFT UAR** | **Strengths:**<br><br>**Weaknesses:** | **Goals** |
| **Test-Taking**<br><br>**TST UAR** | **Strengths:**<br><br>**Weaknesses:** | **Goals** |
| **Time Management**<br><br>**TST UAR** | **Strengths:**<br><br>**Weaknesses:** | **Goals** |
| **Oral Communication**<br><br>**INFP SMI ANX ATT UAR** | **Strengths:**<br><br>**Weaknesses:** | **Goals** |
| **Motivation/Growth Mindset**<br><br>**MOT ANX ATT** | **Strengths:**<br><br>**Weaknesses:** | **Goals** |

Incorporate your LASSI scores into the goal chart to see how they relate to your goals, strengths and weaknesses. Do this for each goal area of the chart.

For example, your SMI (Selecting Main Ideas) and INFP (Information Processing) scores on the LASSI will also give you an idea of how you compare with other college readers. Write these scores in the reading category. If these scores are low, the reading strategies of this text/course will give you specific strategies to help you to grow and improve in reading. Set goals based on what you know of your past experiences, strengths, weaknesses and that you believe will best address your needs.

**Example:** Learn new reading strategies to improve in critical reading and use them to annotate texts effectively to become an active reader in my literature course.

## Activity Five: Campus Connections

Your campus has invested in valuable resources to help you find success with many of these goals that you have just set for yourself. These resources are gold mines. Unfortunately, many students don't find them until it is too late. They have either already met failure, resulting in a Grade Point Average (GPA) that needs to be rebuilt. Or, they are nearing the end of the academic career and wish they would have found the resources sooner. Students who connect with these resource people and support services early in their college careers report high levels of academic success. Successful students seek out support and use it! They realize that the resources are for everyone and for all levels of learning. They are not shy about seeking support. You shouldn't be either! Use the following Campus Resource Sheet (See Figure 1.4 Campus Connections) to seek out the support that is available to you on your campus and connect with the key people who can help you succeed. Make a plan to connect with them this week or next week and use their services frequently! Who knows—you might even end up becoming one of their employees. As a director and supervisor of a learning center who hires and trains academic coaches, I can tell you that I often hire the students who utilize the learning center because the students who use the services at the learning center are often the best and most successful students!

## Figure 1.4: Campus Connections

Most campuses invest in these resources to help students succeed. Search your college website to find these campus resources. Use the chart to write down the contact information, hours, services provided, and appointment time that you set up, and notes from your meetings and visits. Also, be sure to write the appointments you make in your planner.

| Campus Resources | Typical Services Provided | Visit |
|---|---|---|
| **Career Center**<br>Contact person/director:<br><br>**Services Students might be interested in:**<br>• Guidance in choosing a major<br>• Information about internships<br>• Personality tests<br>• Help with resumes and cover letters<br>• Mock Interviews<br>• Career Fairs<br><br>**Location:**<br><br>**Hours:**<br><br>**How to make an appointment:**<br><br>**Phone Number:**<br><br>**Email:** | Career centers typically guide you in finding a major. They might offer a test such as the FOCUS that identifies potential careers that fit with your personality type. The also offer help with finding internships, writing resumes and cover letters, and searching for jobs.<br><br>While some students wait until their senior year to visit the career center, this is a BIG MISTAKE! Students need to start creating a resume right away and begin figuring out what should be on the resume, so they can begin getting those experiences during their first year. Otherwise—they will find they have a lot of empty spaces on their resume when they begin writing it their senior year. | Appointment date(s):<br><br>Notes from visit: |

## Figure 1.4: Campus Connections (*Continued*)

<table>
<tr>
<td>Counseling Center<br>Contact person/director:<br><br>Services Students might be interested in:<br>• Guidance in choosing a major<br>• Personality tests<br>• Help with roommate issues<br>• Sorting out relationship issues<br>• Dealing with anxiety<br>• Coping with stress<br>• Making big life decisions<br>• Resolving conflicts<br>• Just someone who will listen objectively<br>• Dealing with and identifying depression<br><br>Location:<br><br>Hours:<br><br>How to make an appointment:<br><br>Phone Number:<br><br>Email:</td>
<td>Students often make the mistake of thinking that the counseling center is only a place to go if you have mental illness. This is not true at all. In fact, the counseling center is not equipped to deal with mental illness. Rather, the counseling center is a resource for all students. It offers them caring and educated resource people who are available to listen to their needs and help them make sound decisions. It is a place to go when you need an objective listener—someone who can help you resolve conflicts, find coping strategies for stress and anxiety, mild bouts of depression, and making sound decisions. The counseling center is a place to go to get a better understanding of yourself! Successful students do not hesitate to use it when they need someone to offer them sound advice and coping strategies. They realize it is a resource for everyone.</td>
<td>Appointment date(s):<br><br><br>Notes from visit:</td>
</tr>
</table>

## Figure 1.4: Campus Connections (*Continued*)

| | | |
|---|---|---|
| **Campus Ministry**<br>Contact person/director:<br><br>**Services Students might be interested in:**<br>• Spiritual direction and guidance<br>• Worship and prayer services<br>• Scripture sharing and book groups<br>• Retreats<br>• Community outreach and service projects<br>• Social Justice groups<br><br>**Location:**<br><br>**Hours:**<br><br>**How to make and appointment:**<br><br>**Phone Number:**<br><br>**Email:** | Students sometimes forget that academic success depends on more than just studying. It requires that you tend to all of your needs. As a person, you also have spiritual needs. This is true regardless of your religious affiliation. Even people who do not believe in an afterlife have spiritual needs. Spirituality in its simplest forms means tending to your personal wellbeing. A director of a campus ministry center can help you identify and meet your spiritual needs while you are on campus. | Appointment date(s):<br><br>Notes from visit or meetings: |

## Figure 1.4: Campus Connections (*Continued*)

<table>
<tr>
<td>Writing Center<br>Contact person/director:<br><br>Services Students might be interested in:<br>• Help in finding a topic<br>• Feedback on writing<br>• Tips for editing and proofreading<br>• Help with documentation<br><br>Location:<br><br>Hours:<br><br>How to make an appointment:<br><br>Phone Number:<br><br>Email:</td>
<td>One visit to the Writing Center, and you will be convinced it is essential for all of your papers. A Writing Center can help you with all stages of your papers and will make you a stronger writer. All writers seek feedback from others. Many writers pay for feedback. While you are in college, you get this feedback and guidance for free from your Writing Center! Use it—successful students do!</td>
<td>Appointment date(s):<br><br><br>Notes from visit or meetings:</td>
</tr>
</table>

## Figure 1.4: Campus Connections (*Continued*)

<table>
<tr>
<td>Academic Learning Center<br>Contact person/director:<br><br>Services Students might be interested in:<br>◆ Study strategies<br>◆ College reading strategies<br>◆ Test-taking strategies<br>◆ Note-Taking Strategies<br>◆ Time Management Strategies<br>◆ Tutoring<br>◆ Study Groups and Supplemental Instruction<br><br>Location:<br><br>Hours:<br><br>How to make an appointment:<br><br>Phone Number:<br><br>Email:</td>
<td>The Learning Center might be one of THE most important places on campus. It offers resources that could help you improve with all of the skill areas that are key to you achieving the goals you set for the semester. Successful students do not wait until they are struggling to go to the learning center. They go there at the beginning of the semester and continue throughout. They attend all study sessions attached to classes regularly. They utilize every support service available to them—that is why they succeed!</td>
<td>Appointment date(s):<br><br><br>Notes from visit or meetings:</td>
</tr>
</table>

## Figure 1.4: Campus Connections (*Continued*)

<table>
<tr>
<td>Library<br>Contact person/director:<br><br>Services Students might be interested in:<br>• Help in narrowing a topic<br>• Help in researching a topic<br>• Guidance in citing sources<br>• Support in finding relevant sources for a paper<br>• Quiet places for studying and working on course work<br><br>Location:<br><br>Hours:<br><br>How to make an appointment:<br><br>Phone Number:<br><br>Email:</td>
<td>The library is the Academic Hub of your campus. There, you can find trained research consultants who can save you a lot of time in your research. The library staff is also often trained in source citations. Additionally, it has great hidden corners for studying and getting a lot of work finished. Visit it often and use it well. It is a valuable resource.</td>
<td>Appointment date(s):<br><br>Notes from visit or meetings:</td>
</tr>
</table>

## Week Two

# Managing Time & Overcoming Procrastination

Not managing time effectively can lead even the most intelligent and talented person to failure. Time is something we are all given equally, but not all of us manage it effectively. Developing an effective time management system is essential to succeed not only academically but also in life. But how do you do that? There are many different methods, and it will be important for you to personalize your own method. But all successful methods manage time on both a macro and a micro level. Additionally, all successful time management systems take into consideration the multiple roles that you play in your life. While you are a student, you might also be an athlete, an employee, a friend, a boyfriend/girlfriend, spouse, mother/father, daughter, son, brother, sister, and so on. Our lives are multifaceted and have many responsibilities with many tasks. When we only account for time in one role and for tasks in one role, we fail in our roles and tasks. This affects our self-esteem and personal well-being and will also affect the success in all our roles. Thus, it is essential that we take all our roles into account when we manage our time. We want balance and success not chaos and failure. This week's activities will help you to find that balance.

## Activity One: Big Picture Planning—The Macro Level

### Fall Undergraduate Planner, Weeks 1–8

| Week | Monday | Tuesday | Wednesday | Thursday | Friday | Saturday | Sunday |
|---|---|---|---|---|---|---|---|
| 1 | | | | | | | |
| 2 | | | | | | | |
| 3 | | | | | | | |
| 4 | | | | | | | |
| 5 | | | | | | | |
| 6 | | | | | | | |
| 7 | | | | | | | |
| 8 | | | | | | | |

## Fall Undergraduate Planner, Weeks 9–16

| Week | Monday | Tuesday | Wednesday | Thursday | Friday | Saturday | Sunday |
|---|---|---|---|---|---|---|---|
| 9 | | | | | | | |
| 10 | | | | | | | |
| 11 | | | | | | | |
| 12 | | | | | | | |
| 13 | | | | | | | |
| 14 | | | | | | | |
| 15 | | | | | | | |
| 16 | | | | | | | |
| FINALS | | | | | | | |

## Activity One: Big Picture Planning—The Macro Level

### Spring Undergraduate Planner, Weeks 1–8

| Week | Monday | Tuesday | Wednesday | Thursday | Friday | Saturday | Sunday |
|---|---|---|---|---|---|---|---|
| 1 | | | | | | | |
| 2 | | | | | | | |
| 3 | | | | | | | |
| 4 | | | | | | | |
| 5 | | | | | | | |
| 6 | | | | | | | |
| 7 | | | | | | | |
| 8 | | | | | | | |

## Spring Undergraduate Planner, Weeks 9–16

| Week | Monday | Tuesday | Wednesday | Thursday | Friday | Saturday | Sunday |
|---|---|---|---|---|---|---|---|
| 9 | | | | | | | |
| 10 | | | | | | | |
| 11 | | | | | | | |
| 12 | | | | | | | |
| 13 | | | | | | | |
| 14 | | | | | | | |
| 15 | | | | | | | |
| 16 | | | | | | | |
| FINALS | | | | | | | |

**Suggested use of the Long Term Planner**

Use the following steps and this calendar:

1. Number each week of the calendar (1–16), so that you always know what week you are on as the semester progresses.
2. Go through each syllabus and pull out the big assignments/projects and tests (not the daily assignments). Put these on the calendar. You might decide to color code each class. For example, you could highlight your Sociology Class assignments and tests purple, your Nursing tests Pink, and your Psychology Papers and Tests green.
3. If you are an athlete, add all your games to the calendar.
4. If you are a mother/father, add the days that your child is off school or doctor appointments for your child or other dates you need to remember for your children (games, concerts, big events).
5. If you need to travel for work, add that to the calendar.
6. For each of your roles, add the important dates you need to remember this semester. For example, you might be in a wedding or a family member may be having a surgery.

Once you have all the dates plotted out on the calendar, look at what conflicts or advance planning might be necessary and begin that planning now. For example, if you are an athlete and notice that you will be out of town at a game on a date that a test will be given in class, you will need to let your professor know now so that arrangements can be made in advance. Or, if a major paper is due the same week that your father is scheduled to have open-heart surgery, you should discuss this with your professor now so that you can plan ahead and make arrangements in advance. Letting the professor know on the day of the test or the day the paper is due will be too late. The outcome will only result in you losing points or failing because you did not plan ahead. Looking at everything together on one calendar allows you to plan in advance so that you can maintain balance and find success.

## Activity Two: Creating a Study Schedule—More Macro-Level Planning

Successful students create routines for studying. They map out a regular plan for tending to their classes each day. Universally, it is expected that students spend 2–3 hours outside of class per week studying and working on their courses for every hour they spend in class. This means that for a three-credit course students are expected to spend 6–9 hours each week outside of class studying and working on that class. Most students enroll in about 15 credits per semester. When one does the math, it quickly becomes apparent that being a student is a full-time job. And, to be successful, students need to treat studying and academic coursework as a full-time job. Employees map out their work in planners and calendars in order to be successful. Students will also need to do this in order to be successful. To begin this type of planning, create a study schedule (similar to the one in Figure 2.1) for yourself by following the steps below:

1. On the schedule, map out everything that is already fixed (class times, work hours, practice times, meal times, sleep, etc.). Label the items specifically. For example, write which class it is in the time slot.
2. Create study slots totaling 2–3 hours per credit hour for each class you are taking. For example, you should have 6–9 hours mapped out each week for a three-credit-hour class.
    a. Avoid study blocks that are longer than 2 hours. Concentration is diminished after 2 hours. Some students may only be able to focus for 1 hour at a time.
    b. When possible, study right before class or right after class.
    c. Don't create study sessions that you know you will not keep. For example, if you never get up early, do not create an early morning study session.
3. Effective time management allows adequate time for all your needs!
    a. Make sure that you are getting enough sleep. You should have at least 8 hours each night.
    b. You should be scheduling time for three meals a day.
    c. Allow time for physical activity. Physical activity reduces stress and increases cognitive functioning. Scheduling exercise before a difficult class or study session can actually boost your academic performance.
    d. Be social. Reward yourself for getting things done by hanging out with friends. Or, tend to social needs by studying with your friends. Group study is especially effective.
    e. Take time for spiritual needs, reflection, and self-renewal. You need to get away and have some time to yourself. You can combine this with physical activity by going for a walk or run while reflecting, meditating, and praying. Or, maybe just sitting outside in the sun while eating your lunch is what you need. The point is that effective time management often meets multiple needs at once—but it never neglects needs!
4. Color code your schedule. Designate a color for each category and color each block for easy recognition. For example, classes might be pink, study sessions purple, sleep blue, and exercise yellow, and so on.

## Figure 2.1: Create Study Schedule

| Time | Monday | Tuesday | Wednesday | Thursday | Friday | Saturday | Sunday |
|---|---|---|---|---|---|---|---|
| 5:00 a.m. | | | | | | | |
| 6:00 a.m. | | | | | | | |
| 7:00 a.m. | | | | | | | |
| 8:00 a.m. | | | | | | | |
| 9:00 a.m. | | | | | | | |
| 10:00 a.m. | | | | | | | |
| 11:00 a.m. | | | | | | | |
| 12:00 p.m. | | | | | | | |
| 1:00 p.m. | | | | | | | |
| 2:00 p.m. | | | | | | | |
| 3:00 p.m. | | | | | | | |
| 4:00 p.m. | | | | | | | |
| 5:00 p.m. | | | | | | | |
| 6:00 p.m. | | | | | | | |
| 7:00 p.m. | | | | | | | |
| 8:00 p.m. | | | | | | | |
| 9:00 p.m. | | | | | | | |
| 10:00 p.m. | | | | | | | |
| 11:00 p.m. | | | | | | | |
| 12:00 a.m. | | | | | | | |
| 1:00 a.m. | | | | | | | |
| 2:00 a.m. | | | | | | | |
| 3:00 a.m. | | | | | | | |
| 4:00 a.m. | | | | | | | |

## Activity Three: Getting Organized

One of the best ways to same time and find success is to create an organization system for yourself. When working with students, I often find that their organization system consists of one folder and one notebook in which they keep all syllabi, handouts, and notes. When we meet to work on papers and projects or study for exams and I ask to see the assignment guidelines or their notes, they spend 15 minutes trying to find them—and often times they can't find them. Not only does this waste time, it affects their ability to succeed. Taking the time to create an organization system that works for you at the beginning of the semester, can save you a lot of time and improve your grades—and reduce stress.

Below is a chart with some organization tips that tend to work. Look through the list then respond to the reflection questions to find a system that might work for you this semester:

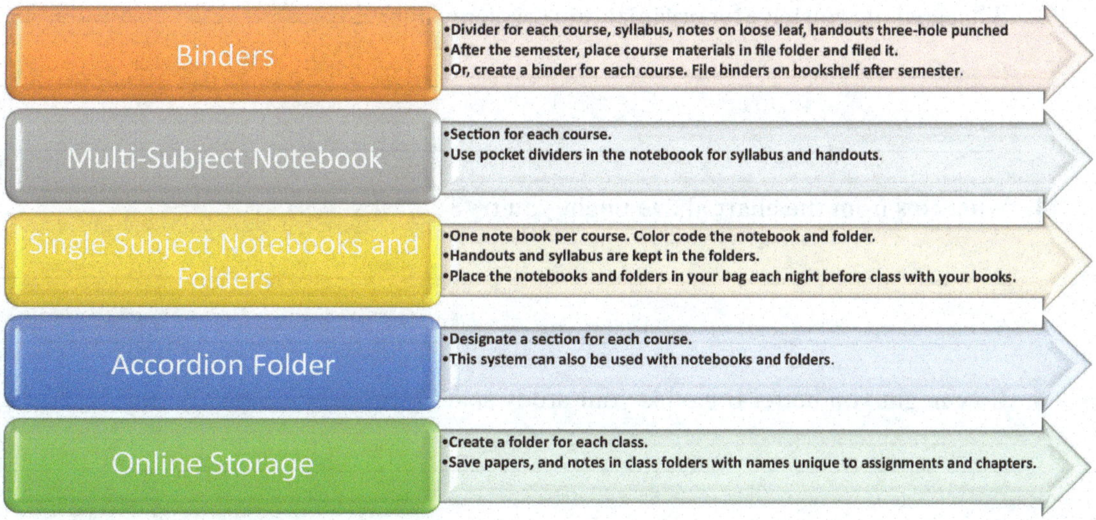

## Questions for Reflection

1. What did you do to stay organized last semester? ____________________

2. How did organization impact your success? ____________________

3. What goals do you have for organization this semester? ____________________

4. What tips from the chart above might you try? ____________________

5. How might you better organize your study space? ____________________

## Activity Four: Creating a To-Do List—Micro Planning

At the beginning of each week, you should set aside about 30 minutes of time to plan for the upcoming week. Some students like to do this on Sunday evenings—other students prefer to do it on Monday mornings. You will need to find the time that works best for you. But, it will be important that you find that time.

1. During those 30 minutes, list each of your roles and look at your long term (semester planner) and syllabi to map out your week. While you go through each role, jot down the tasks that you need to complete during the week. For example, in your role as a student, you will list your assignments for the week for each course. As a family member, you might need to take your grandmother to the doctor or remember to call your mom. Don't forget your spiritual and personal wellness needs. There are boxes for you to list those each week also. While you are listing, don't worry about priority or when you will do it; in the listing phase, you are just listing—getting it all down on paper. As you look at the long-term planner in your role as a student, look about 3 weeks ahead. Papers, projects, and tests that are about 3 weeks out should be hitting your "To-Do" list now so that you can break them into steps and avoid last minute cramming, researching, and writing that sabotag the brightest of students. Also, don't forget the tasks in your roles outside of school, such as laundry, grocery shopping, mowing the lawn, hall meetings, and so on.
2. Once you have completed your list, look at your study schedule and planner and begin to map out your week. Put your daily assignments for classes in the slots in your planner you have designated in your study schedule.
   - For example, your study schedule might show that you will work on your Sociology Class from 2 to 3:30 on Mondays, Wednesdays, and Fridays. And, your "To-Do" list might have read Chapter 3 of Sociology text and respond to discussion board question on it. In your planner, for Monday at 2–3:30 you would write read Chapter 3, Sociology and Discussion Board post.
   - Do this for each item on your "To-Do" list until everything on the list has a place in your planner.
3. Each day, follow your planner. Cross of tasks as you complete them and reward yourself for a job well done.
4. The planning sheet also allows for you to note the strategies you will use to accomplish your tasks—as well as the campus resources you might use. This is important. Mindful and successful students use effective strategies and resources. As you work through the weeks, you will learn strategies to use. For example, for reading an article for a class, you might use "create a concept map of the article as a reading strategy. You might use the Academic Learning Center as a resource. These planning sheets will appear at the end of each week for you to map out your week and begin each week with a goal and gratitude.

As long as you follow your plan, everything should get accomplished for the week. The key is to stick to your plan!

## Weekly Goals

**Week of:** ______________________

**What am I grateful for?**

**What are your goal(s) for the week?**

| **Course:** | ________ | ________ | ________ | ________ | ________ | ________ |
|---|---|---|---|---|---|---|
| • To do: | | | | | | |
| • Strateg(ies): | | | | | | |
| • Resource(s): | | | | | | |

**Personal Wellness/Spirituality:**

**Family & Friends:**

**Weekly Planner** **Week of:** ____________________

| | Monday | Tuesday | Wednesday | Thursday | Friday | Saturday | Sunday |
|---|---|---|---|---|---|---|---|
| 06:00 am | | | | | | | |
| 06:30 am | | | | | | | |
| 07:00 am | | | | | | | |
| 07:30 am | | | | | | | |
| 08:00 am | | | | | | | |
| 08:30 am | | | | | | | |
| 09:00 am | | | | | | | |
| 09:30 am | | | | | | | |
| 10:00 am | | | | | | | |
| 10:30 am | | | | | | | |
| 11:00 am | | | | | | | |
| 11:30 am | | | | | | | |
| 12:00 pm | | | | | | | |
| 12:30 pm | | | | | | | |
| 01:00 pm | | | | | | | |
| 01:30 pm | | | | | | | |
| 02:00 pm | | | | | | | |
| 02:30 pm | | | | | | | |
| 03:00 pm | | | | | | | |
| 03:30 pm | | | | | | | |
| 04:00 pm | | | | | | | |
| 04:30 pm | | | | | | | |
| 05:00 pm | | | | | | | |
| 05:30 pm | | | | | | | |
| 06:00 pm | | | | | | | |
| 06:30 pm | | | | | | | |
| 07:00 pm | | | | | | | |
| 07:30 pm | | | | | | | |
| 08:00 pm | | | | | | | |
| 08:30 pm | | | | | | | |
| 09:00 pm | | | | | | | |
| 09:30 pm | | | | | | | |
| 10:00 pm | | | | | | | |
| 10:30 pm | | | | | | | |

## Activity Five: Overcoming Procrastination

While time management is important and leads to greater organization and success, research is showing it often has very little to do with procrastination. Students who struggle with procrastination often avoid assignments, studying, and tasks because of the emotions associated with them. It has much less to do with knowing how to allocate the appropriate amount of time and create a time management plan.

1. Read the following articles to learn more about how emotional regulation contributes to procrastination.
   - https://www.bbc.com/worklife/article/20200121-why-procrastination-is-about-managing-emotions-not-time
   - https://www.psychologicalscience.org/observer/why-wait-the-science-behind-procrastination
   - https://www.washingtonpost.com/news/wonk/wp/2016/04/27/why-you-cant-help-read-this-article-about-procrastination-instead-of-doing-your-job/
   - https://jamesclear.com/procrastination
2. As you read each article, take some notes using the chart.
3. Finally, synthesize your notes and create some action steps to overcome areas where procrastination is embedding your success.
4. Note the action step on your weekly Mindful Planning sheet.

| Article | Personal Connections/ Where you Related to the Article | New Discoveries about Procrastination | Where the Authors Agreed | Differences in Articles | Action Steps to Take to Overcome Procrastination |
| --- | --- | --- | --- | --- | --- |
| | | | | | |
| | | | | | |
| | | | | | |
| | | | | | |

POSITIVE
MIND. VIBES. LIFE.

**Campus Connection:** The Counseling Center on campus is an excellent resource for finding strategies for regulating emotions and/or uncovering emotions that might be contributing to procrastination.

## Important Thoughts / Things to Remember / Doodling

Week Three

# Evaluating Your Emotional Intelligence

It turns out that the story about the Little Engine who thought he could is really more than an entertaining children's story. It tells us a lot about our own learning. Like the Little Engine, we need to believe we can learn in order to learn. Bandura (1994) and Marzano's (2001) research revealed that in order for learning to take place our self-system must first be engaged and have a positive self-efficacy. We must not only believe we can learn but we must also find the learning to be important. If these conditions are not present, learning will not happen. It doesn't matter how effective and talented the professor is in the classroom. Learning must first begin with us. To ensure that we have the necessary efficacy and attitude to learn, we must work on our emotional intelligence (EI).

What is EI? Our EI is made up of five competencies (Bar-On, 2006)

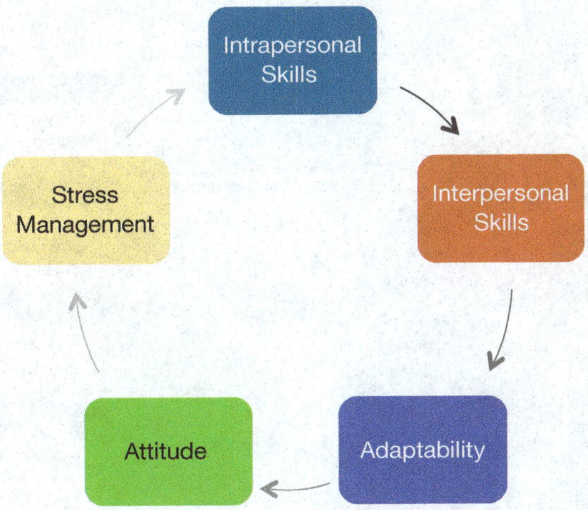


To get a better sense of your EI, this week's activities will challenge you to assess yourself in each of these categories.

## Activity One: Intrapersonal Skills

The chart below shows that intrapersonal skills rely on self-respect, self-awareness, self-reliance, self-love, and self-actualization. Read through the definitions for each of the terms. After careful reflection, assess yourself for each one. For the areas where you are 3 or lower, journal about why you are low in this area and make a plan for improving. What could you do to improve? Is there a resource on campus that could help? For example, you might set up an appointment with the counseling center, campus ministry center, academic learning center, or writing center.

Self-respect (1–5) ______________________________

Plan for improvement ______________________________

Self-awareness (1–5) ______________________________

Plan for improvement ______________________________

Self-reliance (1–5) ______________________________

Plan for improvement ______________________________

Self-love (1–5) ______________________________

Plan for improvement ______________________________

Self-actualization (1–5) ______________________________

Plan for improvement ______________________________

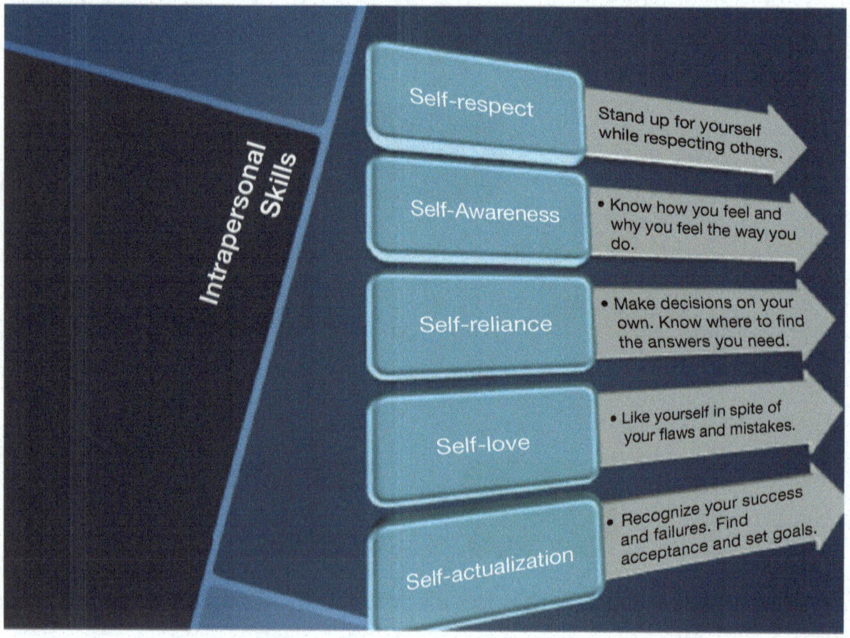

## Activity Two: Interpersonal Skills

Your interpersonal skills help you work well with others. The three main competencies to work on in this area are: social responsibility, collaboration, and empathy.

Reflect on how well you do in this area. When you work with others, are you able to empathize. In other words, do you step in their shoes and imagine how they feel? Are you able to collaborate with others on projects? Are you a team player? What about social responsibility? Do you see yourself connected to a larger community and reflect on how you can make a difference for others? Your answers to these questions say a lot about your interpersonal skills.

Rate yourself in each area:

Social responsibility (1–5) ______________________________

Plan for improvement ______________________________

Collaboration (1–5) ______________________________

Plan for improvement ______________________________

Empathy (1–5) ______________________________

Plan for improvement ______________________________

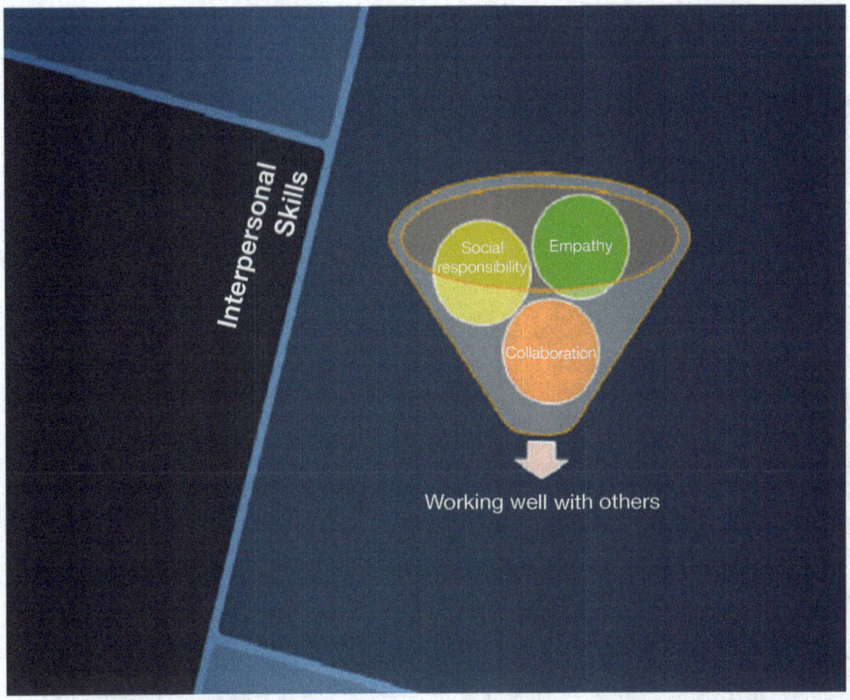

## Activity Three: Adaptability

How adaptable are you? When things don't go as you expect, do you have a meltdown or can you go with the flow and find an alternate plan? Successful students learn how to adapt by implementing reality checks with their thinking to make sure it is logical; they are flexible when plans do not go smoothly, and they know how to problem solve to find alternate plans.

Assess yourself in each of these areas to see how adaptable you are.

**Reality checks**—When you become emotionally upset, how likely are you to question your thoughts and feelings to see if they are logical? 1 (very unlikely) 2 (not likely) 3 (sometimes) 4 (likely) 5 (very likely)

**Flexibility**—When plans change, what is your emotional response? 1 (very anxious) 2 (somewhat anxious) 3 (a little upset) 4 (I figure out a new plan) 5 (excited by the opportunity for something new)

**Problem solving**—In the midst of a conflict, how do you typically respond? 1 (I can't cope with this) 2 (This really sucks) 3 (I find someone who can help) 4 (I take a deep breath and begin to gather resources) 5 (I confidently gather the resources around me and work to find a solution)

Tally your scores to each of these. 9 or lower shows that you might need to work on your adaptability. Which of these areas is your weakest? What resources are available on campus to help you improve in this area? ____________________

What is one step you could take this week to improve in this area of your EI?

____________________

____________________

____________________

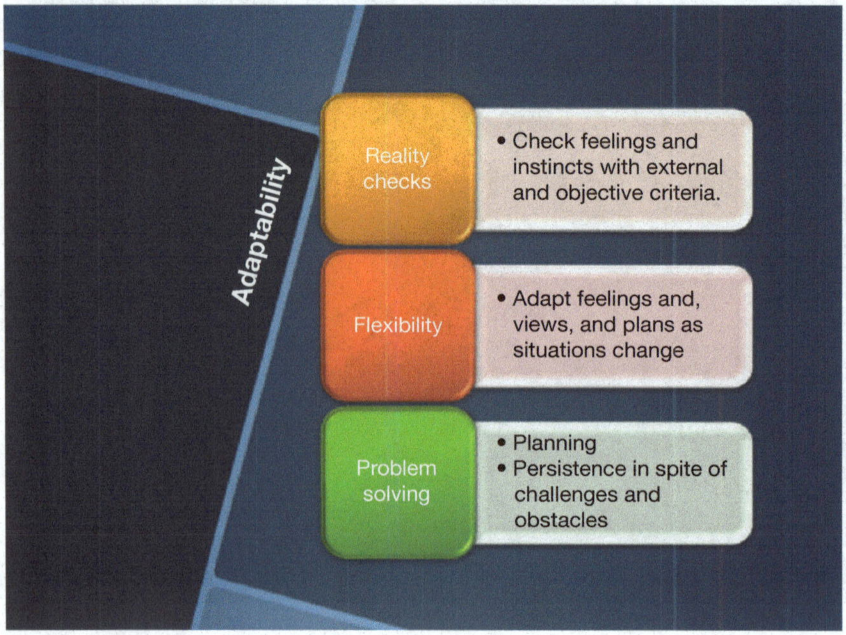

## Activity Four: Stress Management

Many students struggle with stress management. Stress affects all of us. Stress is present in all of our lives and is necessary to help us succeed. It is when stress becomes overwhelming and isn't effectively managed that it becomes detrimental and makes us physically and emotionally ill. When stress affects us on these levels, we become depressed and can't succeed. It is important that we don't allow stress to negatively impact us to these extremes.

1. Look at each key indicator of stress management below and assess yourself from 1 to 5 (1 low and 5 high). What is your tolerance level? What is your impulse control?
2. Make a plan for improving in each of these areas this week. What is one thing you can do to improve in your stress management? What resources are available to help you? For example, could you work out at the fitness center? Make an appointment at the counseling center?

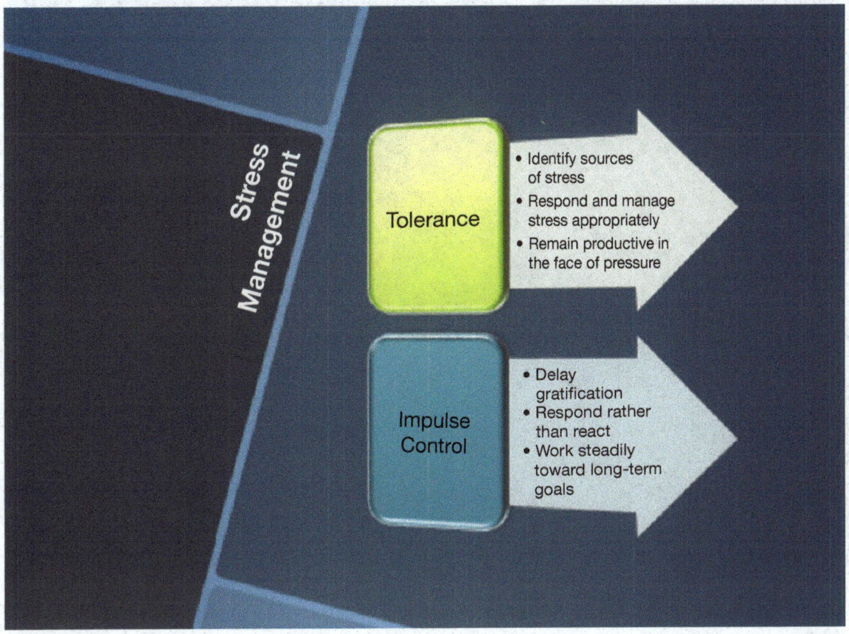


## Activity Five: Attitude

How is your attitude? Your overall attitude has a lot to do with your success. Our thoughts control our actions, so it is important to monitor them and keep them in check. As you go through the day, do you look at what is going well in your life and what you are doing well? Or do you tend to focus on the negative and what is not going well? Focusing only on the negative will not result in a positive and successful attitude. Happy people tend to see the positive in life. And, happy people tend to be more successful.

Mark an X in between the words below to show where you are on the spectrums right now.

Optimism Pessimism

Happy Depressed

What could you do to improve your attitude this week? What resources are available to help you with this?

______________________________________________________________________

______________________________________________________________________

______________________________________________________________________

______________________________________________________________________

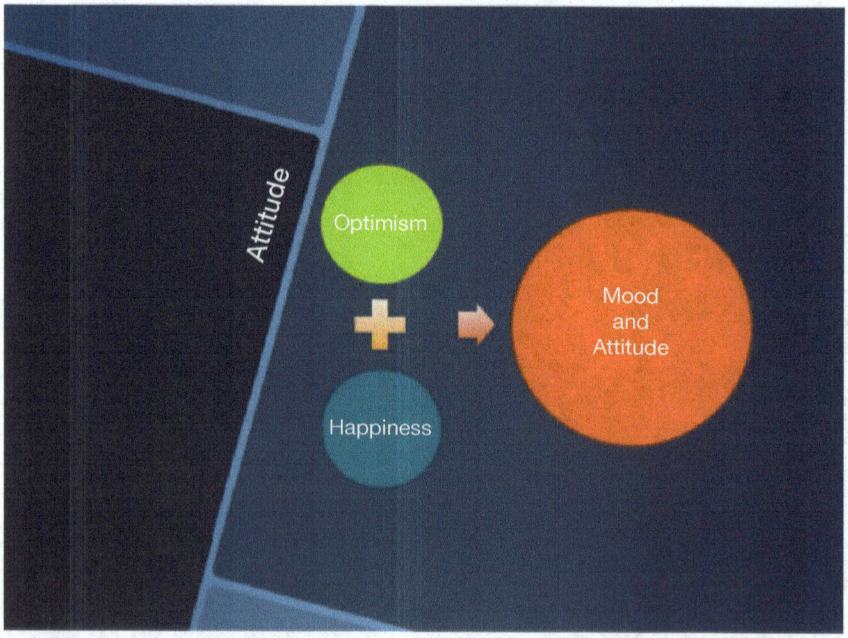


## Activity Six

Now that you have assessed yourself in each of the five competencies of EI and reflected on what you might do this week to improve in each area, set some specific and measurable goals and a plan for improving the competencies that you need the most work on. For example, if stress management is your weakest area, you might set a goal for stress management. See the visual below for some specific goals and a plan for stress management and ways you might assess that goal.

Competency: ____________________________________________

Goal: ____________________________________________

Plan: ____________________________________________

____________________________________________

Assessment measure: ____________________________________________

Competency: ____________________________________________

Goal: ____________________________________________

Plan: ____________________________________________

____________________________________________

Assessment measure: ____________________________________________

## References

Bandura, A. (1994). Self-efficacy. In V. S. Ramachaudran (Ed.), *Encyclopedia of human behavior* (Vol. 4, pp. 71–81). New York: Academic Press. Retrieved from http://www.des.emory.edu/mfp/BanEncy.html

Bar-On, R. (2006). The Bar-On model of emotional-social intelligence (ESI). *Psicothema*. 18(13–25): 21.

Marzano, R. J. (2001). *Designing a new taxonomy of educational objectives*. Thousand Oaks, CA: Corwin Press.

## Weekly Goals

**Week of:** ______________________

**What am I grateful for?**

**What are your goal(s) for the week?**

| **Course:** | ________ | ________ | ________ | ________ | ________ | ________ |
|---|---|---|---|---|---|---|
| • To do: | | | | | | |
| • Strateg(ies): | | | | | | |
| • Resource(s): | | | | | | |

**Personal Wellness/Spirituality:**

**Family & Friends:**

## Weekly Planner

**Week of:** ______________________

| | Monday | Tuesday | Wednesday | Thursday | Friday | Saturday | Sunday |
|---|---|---|---|---|---|---|---|
| 06:00 am | | | | | | | |
| 06:30 am | | | | | | | |
| 07:00 am | | | | | | | |
| 07:30 am | | | | | | | |
| 08:00 am | | | | | | | |
| 08:30 am | | | | | | | |
| 09:00 am | | | | | | | |
| 09:30 am | | | | | | | |
| 10:00 am | | | | | | | |
| 10:30 am | | | | | | | |
| 11:00 am | | | | | | | |
| 11:30 am | | | | | | | |
| 12:00 pm | | | | | | | |
| 12:30 pm | | | | | | | |
| 01:00 pm | | | | | | | |
| 01:30 pm | | | | | | | |
| 02:00 pm | | | | | | | |
| 02:30 pm | | | | | | | |
| 03:00 pm | | | | | | | |
| 03:30 pm | | | | | | | |
| 04:00 pm | | | | | | | |
| 04:30 pm | | | | | | | |
| 05:00 pm | | | | | | | |
| 05:30 pm | | | | | | | |
| 06:00 pm | | | | | | | |
| 06:30 pm | | | | | | | |
| 07:00 pm | | | | | | | |
| 07:30 pm | | | | | | | |
| 08:00 pm | | | | | | | |
| 08:30 pm | | | | | | | |
| 09:00 pm | | | | | | | |
| 09:30 pm | | | | | | | |
| 10:00 pm | | | | | | | |
| 10:30 pm | | | | | | | |

## Important Thoughts / Things to Remember / Doodling

Week Four

# Identifying Distorted Thoughts

Many of our thought processes are automatic and formed by emotional and physical reactions to our surroundings. Often these thoughts are illogical and cause us unnecessary stress and anxiety. Learning to recognize and challenge these distorted thoughts when they are occurring can reduce our stress and help us to make better choices that are not governed by emotional reactions (Sherman, 2013). In the academic world, identifying and eliminating distorted thinking would likely lead to improved performance in your classes.

| Distorted Thoughts | Examples |
| --- | --- |
| ❖ **Mind reading:** You know what others are thinking about you—and you assume it is bad. | ❖ You didn't read the chapter before class, and you feel the professor assumed this about you when you walked in the classroom and gave you a nasty look. |
| ❖ **Overgeneralization:** One negative event is seen as a pattern. | ❖ You fail a test. So you think: I always fail tests. |
| ❖ **All-or-nothing thinking:** Everything is all good or all bad. If you don't do something perfectly, you fail. | ❖ I got a C on the paper. I am a horrible student. I shouldn't be in college.<br>❖ I got an A on the last test. I will get an A in the class. |

(*Continued*)

| Distorted Thoughts | Examples |
|---|---|
| ❖ **Fortune telling:** You know things will turn out badly. | ❖ You will freeze up in the middle of your presentation—just like you always do. |
| ❖ **Mental filtering:** You only see the negative aspects of life. You always point out what is wrong with things or people. | ❖ There is never anything good to eat in the dining hall. Or, there is nothing good about you. You are too tall, or have the wrong color of hair, or too pale, etc. |
| ❖ **Emotional reasoning:** You think your negative feelings reflect reality. | ❖ You feel bad about your class. So you think: "I didn't understand this assignment. So I am going to fail this course." |
| ❖ **Comparative thinking:** You measure yourself by others' ability and judge yourself accordingly—even though the comparison may be inaccurate. | ❖ Everyone else already finished the test. I have ten problems left. They did better than me. I am going to fail the test. |
| ❖ **Magnification/Minimization:** You blow things out of perspective or don't give things as much significance as you should. | ❖ You fail a quiz that is only ten percent of the course and obsess over it and believe you will fail the entire course. You consider dropping the course because of the quiz. Or, you blow off a major test and don't study because you have been attending class and haven't had any questions. |
| ❖ **Should:** You constantly obsess and dwell on how you believe situations should be rather than the reality of the situation. | ❖ Your professor refuses to provide study guides for your course. You constantly complain about how unfair it is and how a professor SHOULD provide a study guide rather than dealing with the situation in a proactive way by creating your own study guide or organizing a group study session. |
| ❖ **Personalization:** You blame yourself when anything negative happens—even when it is out of your control. Often you feel others are targeting you specifically. | ❖ The professor put those questions on the test because he knew I would never be able to answer them correctly. It is my fault the questions were on the test. |

Source: Chart created using information taken from Sherman (2013).

## Activity One

Read through the types of distorted thoughts in the chart above. Which of the distorted thoughts and examples do you recognize in your life?

______________________________________________________________________

______________________________________________________________________

______________________________________________________________________

When are they most likely to occur? In which situations, do you fall into these faulty paradigms of thought? Why?

______________________________________________________________________

______________________________________________________________________

______________________________________________________________________

______________________________________________________________________

For each distorted thought that you identified, note one specific step you can take to identify and challenge the thought when it occurs

- Distorted thought ______________________ Step ______________________
- Distorted thought ______________________ Step ______________________
- Distorted thought ______________________ Step ______________________
- Distorted thought ______________________ Step ______________________
- Distorted thought ______________________ Step ______________________
- Distorted thought ______________________ Step ______________________
- Distorted thought ______________________ Step ______________________

## Activity Two: Emotional Response Journal

Use the following journal to track and monitor your thinking this week. Each time you have an emotional reaction or find yourself procrastinating or in conflict, begin to journal to the questions so that you can identify the distortions occurring in your thought process and challenge them head on.

**Entry One** **Date** **Time**

What feelings are you experiencing?

What task, event, or activity triggered the feelings?

Describe all your thoughts and feelings about this task/activity/event? Don't worry about the wording and punctuation. Just write your thoughts as they come to you.

Looking back at your responses to the questions above, which distortions can you identify in your writing? Check as many as possible that apply and give examples beside each:

All-or-nothing ______________________________

Overgeneralization ______________________________

Mind reading ______________________________

Fortune telling ______________________________

Magnification/minimization ______________________________

Should ______________________________

Personalization ______________________________

Emotional reasoning ______________________________

Comparative ______________________________

What evidence exists for your thoughts and feelings?

How could you verify your thoughts and feelings? Would it be worth while to do so?

If it is true, what is the worst that could happen? What would you do to cope with it?

How does continuing to believe this and/or dwelling on this affect me?

What are more rational thoughts or reasons for what happened? And/or, what is a plan that you could use to resolve this issue so that you can move on and feel better?

**Entry Two** **Date** **Time**

**What feelings are you experiencing?**

**What task, event, or activity triggered the feelings?**

**Describe all your thoughts and feelings about this task/activity/event? Don't worry about the wording and punctuation. Just write your thoughts as they come to you.**

**Looking back at your responses to the questions above, which distortions can you identify in your writing? Check as many as possible that apply and give examples beside each:**

All-or-nothing ______________________________

Overgeneralization ______________________________

Mind reading ______________________________

Fortune telling ______________________________

Magnification/minimization ______________________________

Should ______________________________

Personalization ______________________________

Emotional reasoning ______________________________

Comparative ______________________________

**What evidence exists for your thoughts and feelings?**

**How could you verify your thoughts and feelings? Would it be worth while to do so?**

**If it is true, what is the worst that could happen? What would you do to cope with it?**

**How does continuing to believe this and/or dwelling on this affect you?**

**What are more rational thoughts or reasons for what happened? And/or, what is a plan that you could use to resolve this issue so that you can move on and feel better?**

## Entry Three Date Time

**What feelings are you experiencing?**

**What task, event, or activity triggered the feelings?**

**Describe all your thoughts and feelings about this task/activity/event? Don't worry about the wording and punctuation. Just write your thoughts as they come to you.**

**Looking back at your responses to the questions above, which distortions can you identify in your writing? Check as many as possible that apply and give examples beside each:**

**All-or-nothing** ______________________________

**Overgeneralization** ______________________________

**Mind reading** ______________________________

**Fortune telling** ______________________________

**Magnification/minimization** ______________________________

**Should** ______________________________

**Personalization** ______________________________

**Emotional reasoning** ______________________________

**Comparative** ______________________________

**What evidence exists for your thoughts and feelings?**

**How could you verify your thoughts and feelings? Would it be worth while to do so?**

**If it is true, what is the worst that could happen? What would you do to cope with it?**

**How does continuing to believe this and/or dwelling on this affect you?**

**What are more rational thoughts or reasons for what happened? And/or, what is a plan that you could use to resolve this issue so that you can move on and feel better?**

## Activity Three: Identifying Distorted Thinking in Others

Sometimes it is easier to identify distorted thinking in other people's lives. Literature offers us a window into other's experiences. It gives us a chance to reflect on the choices, struggles, and conflicts of other people in a way that we learn to empathize and find ways to problem solve. In discussing the characters of stories, we learn to place ourselves in the experiences of others and imagine how we might feel and what we might do if we were in their situation. In discussing these stories with others, we hear how others perceive the situations, as well as how they might feel in that situation and what they might do differently. In college, you read many stories. Choose one of the texts you are currently reading for a course. It might be a common read for a first-year experience course, a short story or book from a literature course, or a book from another course you are reading. Pay attention to the character's thoughts, words, and actions. See if you can identify any cognitive distortions. When you find distorted thinking, note it in the chart below, explain how you identified it, and then offer some advice you would give to the character to challenge the distorted thinking. By practicing identifying distorted thoughts in literature, you will become more adept at recognizing it in yourself and finding ways to challenge it in your life.

***(If you aren't taking a literature course or reading a book with characters in it, identify these thoughts in characters from a TV show or movie while you are watching. Use those examples to complete the chart below.)***

| Distorted Thinking | Example from Literature | Advice for Challenging the Distorted Thought |
|---|---|---|
| ❖ **Mind reading:** You know what others are thinking about you—and you assume it is bad. | | |
| ❖ **Overgeneralization:** One negative event is seen as a pattern. | | |
| ❖ **All-or-nothing thinking:** Everything is all good or all bad. If you don't do something perfectly, you fail. | | |
| ❖ **Fortune telling:** You know things will turn out badly. | | |
| ❖ **Mental filtering:** You only see the negative aspects of life. You always point out what is wrong with things or people. | | |

| Distorted Thinking | Example from Literature | Advice for Challenging the Distorted Thought |
|---|---|---|
| ❖ **Emotional reasoning:** You think your negative feelings reflect reality. | | |
| ❖ **Comparative thinking:** You measure yourself by others ability and judge yourself accordingly—even though the comparison may be inaccurate. | | |
| ❖ **Magnification/ Minimization:** You blows things out of perspective or don't give things as much significance as you should. | | |
| ❖ **Should:** You constantly obsess and dwell on how you believe situations should be rather than the reality of the situation. | | |
| ❖ **Personalization:** You blame yourself when anything negative happens—even when it is out of your control. Often you feel others are targeting you specifically. | | |

## Reference


Sherman, C. (2013). How cognitive therapy can stop negativity. *ADDitude: Living with attention deficit*. Retrieved from http://www.additudemag.com/adhd/article/912-2.html

Failure happens all the time.
It happens every day in practice.
What makes you better
is how you react to it.

**—Mia Hamm**

**Weekly Goals** **Week of:** ____________________

**What am I grateful for?**

**What are your goal(s) for the week?**

| **Course:** | ______ | ______ | ______ | ______ | ______ | ______ |
|---|---|---|---|---|---|---|
| • To do: | | | | | | |
| • Strateg(ies): | | | | | | |
| • Resource(s): | | | | | | |

**Personal Wellness/Spirituality:**

**Family & Friends:**

## Weekly Planner

**Week of:** ________________

| | Monday | Tuesday | Wednesday | Thursday | Friday | Saturday | Sunday |
|---|---|---|---|---|---|---|---|
| 06:00 am | | | | | | | |
| 06:30 am | | | | | | | |
| 07:00 am | | | | | | | |
| 07:30 am | | | | | | | |
| 08:00 am | | | | | | | |
| 08:30 am | | | | | | | |
| 09:00 am | | | | | | | |
| 09:30 am | | | | | | | |
| 10:00 am | | | | | | | |
| 10:30 am | | | | | | | |
| 11:00 am | | | | | | | |
| 11:30 am | | | | | | | |
| 12:00 pm | | | | | | | |
| 12:30 pm | | | | | | | |
| 01:00 pm | | | | | | | |
| 01:30 pm | | | | | | | |
| 02:00 pm | | | | | | | |
| 02:30 pm | | | | | | | |
| 03:00 pm | | | | | | | |
| 03:30 pm | | | | | | | |
| 04:00 pm | | | | | | | |
| 04:30 pm | | | | | | | |
| 05:00 pm | | | | | | | |
| 05:30 pm | | | | | | | |
| 06:00 pm | | | | | | | |
| 06:30 pm | | | | | | | |
| 07:00 pm | | | | | | | |
| 07:30 pm | | | | | | | |
| 08:00 pm | | | | | | | |
| 08:30 pm | | | | | | | |
| 09:00 pm | | | | | | | |
| 09:30 pm | | | | | | | |
| 10:00 pm | | | | | | | |
| 10:30 pm | | | | | | | |

## Important Thoughts / Things to Remember / Doodling

Week Five

# Developing Active Reading Strategies

If you are trying to read your textbooks like a novel, you are probably not getting very far. Most students who read their texts in this manner find themselves reading a few paragraphs before their minds drift off into other thoughts. Once they realize they have drifted, they become frustrated and go back to reread the paragraphs because while their eyes were moving across the page their brain did not comprehend any of the text. So, they begin again—determined to NOT LOSE FOCUS. They may get one additional paragraph read before they find themselves again drifting. Feeling hopeless, they close the book and give up.

The problem with this strategy is that it is passive. Effective reading is active. For reading to be meaningful, the reader and text need to converse and interact with one another. How do you communicate with a text? Easily! You ask it questions and respond to it by marking on it while you read. This is called annotating. In K-12 the books you use in school do not belong to you. So, you are not allowed to mark in them. Unfortunately, this deprives you of learning to read actively—unless you write your notes in a notebook or on sticky notes. Now that you are in college, you own the texts. You paid a lot of money for the textbooks—so make them useful to you. Mark in them! There are many Active Reading Strategies for marking in and interacting with your textbooks. These activities will help you to identify strategies that work for you. The reading situation and your learning style will determine the strategy most appropriate. You cannot use one strategy for all situations. You must determine which strategy best fits the reading situation based on the text, the purpose of your reading, and how you will be assessed over the reading.

## Strategies of Inquiry

Determining your purpose for reading can be confusing at times. In college, students are asked to read and respond to reading through four strategies of inquiry. Identifying how you are being asked to read can help you in knowing what to mark and how to respond in your marking. The chart below gives examples of the four strategies of inquiry, as well as common assignments that use the strategies: reading to explore, reading to explain, reading to evaluate, and reading to reflect. In many cases, assignments will ask you to combine these strategies or to use all four of them.

**Before you read**

- Consult syllabus and notes
- Consult overview sources (fill in gaps/create schema)
  - University Library
  - Google/wikipedia (get a general sense of the topic)

**Ask yourself**

- How will I be assessed over the reading? How should I read? What should I note?
- What sources can I consult? How reliable are they?

**Why are you reading? What do you know?**

| Strategy | Examples |
|---|---|
| • Explore | • What do I notice? How does it contribute meaning? (Literary analysis) |
| • Explain | • What is this saying? What do I have to say about it to others? (Summary/list main points) |
| • Evaluate | • What do I think about this and how it is presented? (Critical review) |
| • Reflect | • How does this compare with my experiences? (Reader Response) |

**Strategies of Inquiry**

## Activity One

- List each of your classes.
- For each class, write down your reading (e.g., textbook, short story, article).
- Besides each reading, list the assignment that is assessing your reading (discussion forum post, quiz, journal reflection, test, paper, and so on).
- Beside the assessment/assignment, list the strategies of inquiry you will use for your reading in order to be successful on the assignment/assessment.

Use the following course (Community Health) examples as a guide:
Course: Community Health

- Book/*Spirituality of Nursing*: Journal (reflect), test (explain, reflect, evaluate)
- Book/*The Spirit Catches You and You Fall*: Presentation (explain, explore), Assessment of Family (all strategies), Journal (all strategies)
- Textbook (explain, evaluate, reflect)
- Online articles (evaluate, reflect, explore)

## Strategies for Active Reading

Students often go to class unprepared. They don't read the textbook or assignment before class because they feel it takes too long or that it is too boring. Unfortunately, that means they spend the entire class period trying to figure out and learn the material the professor is talking about. When you read the chapter and material before class, the class lecture and presentations are not new material. You are already familiar with it because you have read. This makes the class period more meaningful. You can attach meaning to what the professor is discussing and learn the content at a higher level because you have already created a schema or ladder of knowledge to attach the lecture material to during class.

The following reading strategies can help your reading before class more become efficient and effective because they keep you active—they give your reading purpose and focus.

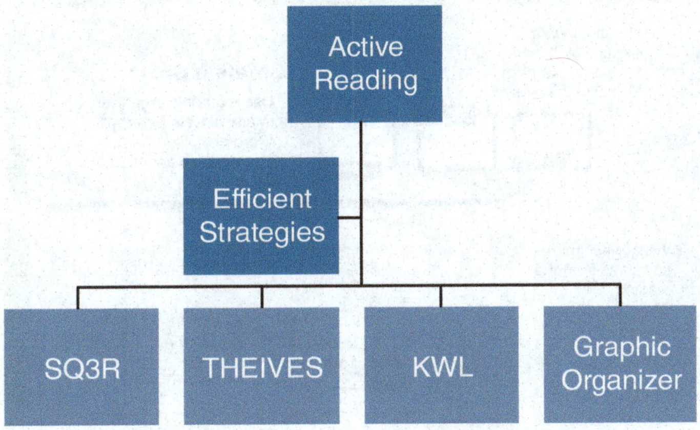

## KWL Method

**KWL** provides students with a strategy for visually depicting what they know, want to know, and have learned.

Know: Before reading a text, quickly scan it. Predict what it will be about and write down everything you already know about it.

Want to know: Look at the assignment guidelines, notes, syllabus outcomes, and goals. What do you want and NEED to know from the chapter. Make a list.

Learn: After reading, make a list and write a quick summary of what you have learned.

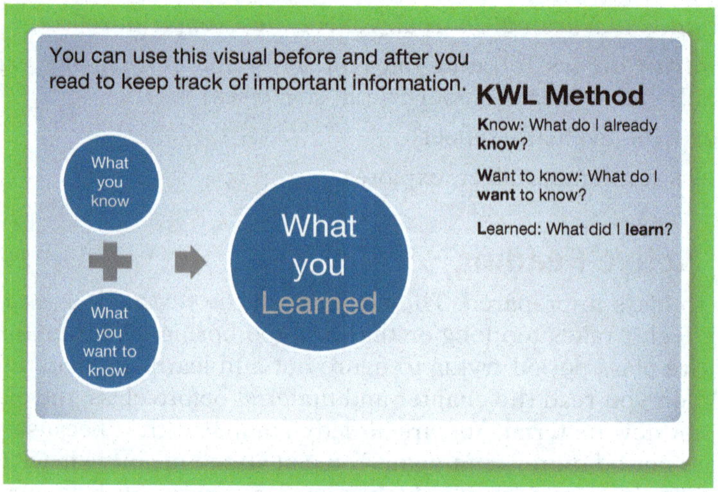


Create charts using SmartArt in Word or PowerPoint.

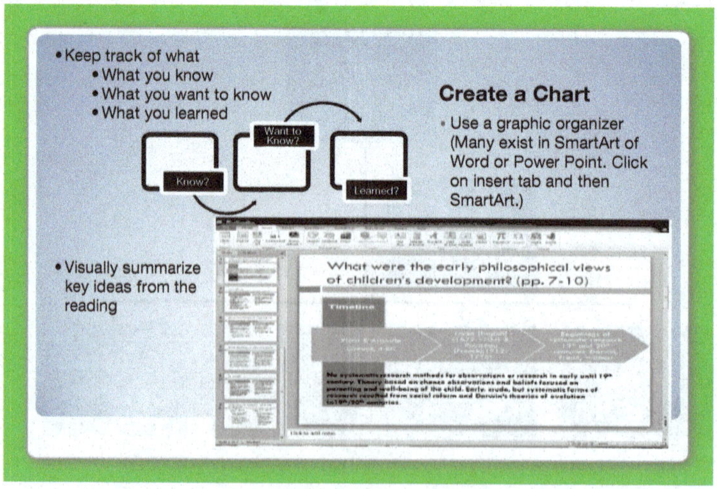

## SQ3R

Survey: Do a quick preview of the chapter. Look at the title, illustrations, vocabulary, end of chapter questions, and the end of chapter summary. Activate your schema by reflecting on what you already know about the chapter and how it fits with the class goals and objectives.

Questions: Turn each major heading into a question. Write it beside the heading.

Read: Quickly read the section below the heading with the purpose of answering the heading question that you created.

Respond: Write a 1–2 sentence response in the margin below the question.

Review: After reading the chapter, re-read your 1–2 sentence responses and use them to write your own, brief, chapter summary.

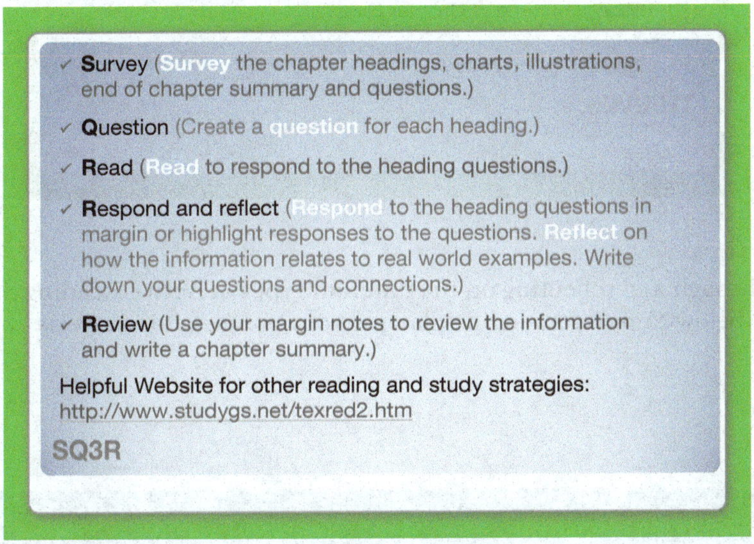


## THIEVES

Much like SQ3R, THIEVES provides a quick and easy process for efficiently pulling key information from textbook chapters. Like a thief, THIEVES allows you to quickly grab the most precious and valuable items needed.

Title: Activate prior knowledge with the title.

Headings: Get a sense of the chapter content by reading headings.

Illustrations: Read and pay attention to all illustrations.

Every first sentence of every paragraph. Reading every first sentence, gives you all of the topic sentences.

Vocabulary: Highlight key vocabulary. Make concept cards for the key vocabulary words you need to learn.

End of chapter questions: Read the end of chapter questions to get a sense of what you should know. See if you can answer them.

Summary: Read the chapter summary. All the key information is in the summary.

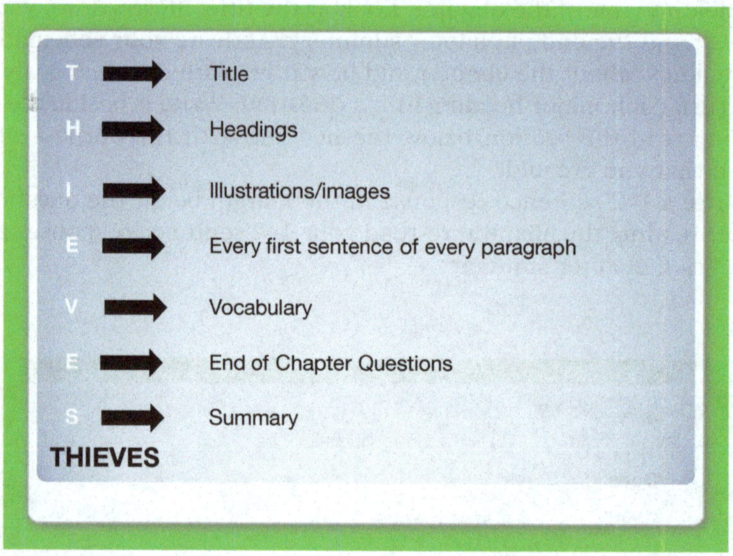


## Activity Two

After reading through and reflecting on the different types of Active Reading Strategies, complete the chart below to make a reading plan for your courses this semester.

| Course | Reading Assignment(s) | Strategy(ies) of Inquiry | Reading Strategies |
|---|---|---|---|
| | | | |
| | | | |
| | | | |
| | | | |
| | | | |
| | | | |

Success is liking yourself,
liking what you do,
and liking how you do it.

**— Maya Angelou**

**Weekly Goals** **Week of:** ____________________

**What am I grateful for?**

**What are your goal(s) for the week?**

| **Course:** | ______ | ______ | ______ | ______ | ______ | ______ |
|---|---|---|---|---|---|---|
| • To do: | | | | | | |
| • Strateg(ies): | | | | | | |
| • Resource(s): | | | | | | |

**Personal Wellness/Spirituality:**

**Family & Friends:**

**Weekly Planner** **Week of:** ____________________

| | Monday | Tuesday | Wednesday | Thursday | Friday | Saturday | Sunday |
|---|---|---|---|---|---|---|---|
| 06:00 am | | | | | | | |
| 06:30 am | | | | | | | |
| 07:00 am | | | | | | | |
| 07:30 am | | | | | | | |
| 08:00 am | | | | | | | |
| 08:30 am | | | | | | | |
| 09:00 am | | | | | | | |
| 09:30 am | | | | | | | |
| 10:00 am | | | | | | | |
| 10:30 am | | | | | | | |
| 11:00 am | | | | | | | |
| 11:30 am | | | | | | | |
| 12:00 pm | | | | | | | |
| 12:30 pm | | | | | | | |
| 01:00 pm | | | | | | | |
| 01:30 pm | | | | | | | |
| 02:00 pm | | | | | | | |
| 02:30 pm | | | | | | | |
| 03:00 pm | | | | | | | |
| 03:30 pm | | | | | | | |
| 04:00 pm | | | | | | | |
| 04:30 pm | | | | | | | |
| 05:00 pm | | | | | | | |
| 05:30 pm | | | | | | | |
| 06:00 pm | | | | | | | |
| 06:30 pm | | | | | | | |
| 07:00 pm | | | | | | | |
| 07:30 pm | | | | | | | |
| 08:00 pm | | | | | | | |
| 08:30 pm | | | | | | | |
| 09:00 pm | | | | | | | |
| 09:30 pm | | | | | | | |
| 10:00 pm | | | | | | | |
| 10:30 pm | | | | | | | |

# Important Thoughts / Things to Remember / Doodling

Week Six

# Identifying Main Points

In working with students, I often hear them say that they believe they are terrible readers. They lack confidence in their ability to comprehend texts. Using the active reading strategies and critical reading strategies help them tremendously! However, some of them lack the basic skill of identifying the structure of writing. They have never learned to look at how paragraphs are organized to see how they are working together to make the main point of the text. Reviewing and identifying the basics of writing structure is an important step toward improving reading comprehension, critical reading, and overall success in college.

Here is a quick review of the basics. Most writing is thesis driven. This means that the thesis (central argument or point of the writing) will come in the opening paragraphs called the introduction. Usually, it will be the last few sentences of the introduction. The thesis will then be supported with paragraphs within the body of the writing. The paragraphs order should be linked back to the organization of the thesis, and they should be directly connected to the thesis. Their function should be to support the thesis.

Each paragraph should have a topic sentence. The topic sentence serves to govern the organization of the paragraph. In essence, the sentences other than the topic sentence should be supporting sentences. Their function is to develop and support the topic sentence. There are many different types of paragraph structures. The structure is determined by the purpose and function of the paragraph. For example, a paragraph might serve as an example, or it might define, or it could be used to narrate or persuade. Knowing the function of the paragraph and its main idea in relation to the thesis is key to helping you comprehend the reading and also in helping you critically evaluate it.

Finally, the conclusion is intended to briefly summarize the main ideas of the text and to leave the reader with something to ponder or think about. It often will draw conclusions or inferences. It might also suggest further needs for research.

## Common Paragraph Structures

- Listing
- Example
- Definition
- Classification
- Chronological order
- Cause–effect
- Comparison/contrast

| Paragraph Structure | Purpose | Signal Words |
|---|---|---|
| **Listing/Examples** | Offers specific instances that illustrate the concept. | For example, to illustrate, to show, the following list, these examples, in other words, namely |
| **Compare and/or Contrast** | Offers similarities and/or differences | Similarly, like, compared, contrarily, in addition to, however, yet, but, although, unlike |
| **Definition** | Give the meaning of a concept | To define, means, that is, punctuation clues: parenthesis, brackets, dashes |
| **Classification** | Shows how a word, idea, object or concept fits within a particular category | To classify, to categorize, within, features, characteristics, parts, types |
| **Chronological Order or Sequence** | Presents the order of steps or events. | Before, after, first, second, third, last, finally, now, since, then, once |
| **Cause-effect** | Shows how events are related or connected | Because, as a result, in relation to, thus, consequently, in the event, therefore |
| **Summary** | Condenses the main ideas | In summary, summing up, briefly, in conclusion |

## Activity One: Noting Writing Structure to Improve Reading Comprehension

For one of your reading assignments, note the structure of the writing. Identify the thesis. Also, identify the topic sentence and paragraph structure for each paragraph in the writing. Finally, use the concept map below or create an electronic concept map using SmartArt in Word (under Insert tab) to reveal the structure of the writing.

Thesis____________________________

Paragraph

- Topic sentence_________________
- Paragraph type

  ______________________________

  ______________________________

Paragraph

- Topic sentence_________________
- Paragraph type

  ______________________________

  ______________________________

Paragraph

- Topic sentence_________________
- Paragraph type

  ______________________________

  ______________________________

Paragraph

- Topic sentence_________________
- Paragraph type

  ______________________________

  ______________________________

Paragraph

- Topic sentence_________________
- Paragraph type

  ______________________________

  ______________________________

Paragraph

- ♦ Topic sentence________________
- ♦ Paragraph type

  ______________________________

  ______________________________

Paragraph

- ♦ Topic sentence________________
- ♦ Paragraph type

  ______________________________

  ______________________________

Paragraph

- ♦ Topic sentence________________
- ♦ Paragraph type

  ______________________________

  ______________________________

Paragraph

- ♦ Topic sentence________________
- ♦ Paragraph type

  ______________________________

  ______________________________

Paragraph

- ♦ Topic sentence________________
- ♦ Paragraph type

  ______________________________

  ______________________________

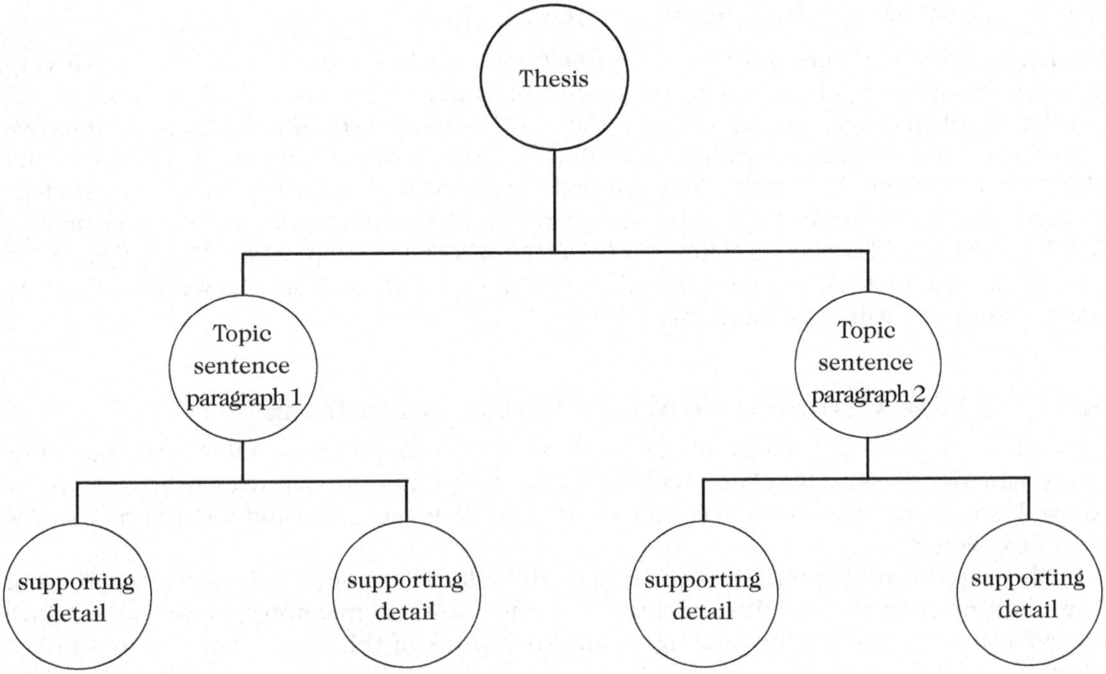


Reflection: How did identifying the structure of the writing affect or improve your understanding of the reading?

_______________________________________________

_______________________________________________

What difficulties or challenges did you encounter with this?

_______________________________________________

_______________________________________________

Where could you go to get further support with this type of reading? (See campus resource sheet in Week One.)

_______________________________________________

_______________________________________________

## The Link between Reading and Vocabulary

Students commonly complain that they aren't good readers because they don't have very strong vocabulary. If you are among these students and feel that your vocabulary is lacking, I will give you the same advice I give to them—READ! Honestly, the best way to improve your vocabulary is through reading—any kind of reading. And when you are reading, don't skip over words you don't know. You can build your vocabulary by (1) using context clues to figure out the meaning, (2) looking them up in a dictionary, (3) learning and using root words, prefixes, and suffixes to figure out the meanings of unknown words. Also, as you learn new words, use them. Challenge yourself to use the word throughout the week so that you don't forget the meaning of the word.

## Activity Two: Common Roots, Prefixes, and Suffixes

As students, you are doing a lot of reading in your courses. In this reading, you encounter many new words each day. This week avoid the temptation to skip over words you don't know. Instead, use the following strategies to learn their meanings and add the new words to your vocabulary.

Choose two roots, prefixes, and suffixes to look for in your reading this week. Note how they apply to the meaning of the words and use their meanings to decipher, figure out what new words in your reading mean. Keep track of the words that you find in the chart.

| Root, Prefix or Suffix | Meaning | Examples |
|---|---|---|
| a, ac, ad, af, ag, al, an, ap, as, at | to, toward, near, in addition to, by | aside, accompany, adjust, aggression, allocate, annihilate, affix, associate, attend, adverb |
| a-, an- | not, without | apolitical, atheist, anarchy, anonymous, apathy, aphasia, anemia |
| ab, abs | away from, off | absolve, abrupt, absent |
| -able, -ible | Adjective: worth, ability | solvable, incredible |
| acer, acid, acri | bitter, sour, sharp | acerbic, acidity, acrid, acrimony |
| act, ag | do, act, drive | active, react, agent, active, agitate |
| acu | sharp | acute, acupuncture, accurate |
| -acy, -cy | Noun: state or quality | privacy, infancy, adequacy, intimacy, supremacy |
| -ade | act, product, sweet drink | blockade, lemonade |
| aer, aero | air, atmosphere, aviation | aerial, aerosol, aerodrome |
| ag, agi, ig, act | do, move, go | agent, agenda, agitate, navigate, ambiguous, action |

| Root, Prefix or Suffix | Meaning | Examples |
|---|---|---|
| -age | Noun: activity, or result of action | courage, suffrage, shrinkage, tonnage |
| agri, agro | pertaining to fields or soil | agriculture, agroindustry |
| -al | Noun: action, result of action | referral, disavowal, disposal, festival |
| -al, -ial, -ical | Adjective: quality, relation | structural, territorial, categorical |
| alb, albo | white, without pigment | albino, albite |
| ali, allo, alter | other | alias, alibi, alien, alloy, alter, alter ego, altruism |
| alt | high, deep | altimeter, altitude |
| am, ami, amor | love, like, liking | amorous, amiable, amicable, enamoured |
| ambi | both | ambidextrous |
| ambul | to walk | ambulatory, amble, ambulance, somnambulist |
| -an | Noun: person | artisan, guardian, historian, magician |
| ana, ano | up, back, again, anew | anode, anagram, anagenetic |
| -ance, -ence | Noun: action, state, quality or process | resistance, independence, extravagance, fraudulence |
| -ancy, -ency | Noun: state, quality or capacity | vacancy, agency, truancy, latency |
| andr, andro | male, characteristics of men | androcentric, android |
| ang | angular | Angle |
| anim | mind, life, spirit, anger | animal, animate, animosity |
| ann, annu, enni | yearly | annual, annuity, anniversary, perennial |
| -ant, -ent | Noun: an agent, something that performs the action | disinfectant, dependent, fragrant |
| -ant, -ent, -ient | Adjective: kind of agent, indication | important, dependent, convenient |
| ante | before | anterior, anteroom, antebellum, antedate, antecedent, antediluvian |
| anthrop | man | anthropology, misanthrope, philanthropy |
| anti, ant | against, opposite | antisocial, antiseptic, antithesis, antibody, antinomies, antifreeze, antipathy |

*(Continued)*

| Root, Prefix or Suffix | Meaning | Examples |
|---|---|---|
| anti, antico | old | antique, antiquated, antiquity |
| apo, ap, aph | away from, detached, formed | apology, apocalypse, aphagia |
| aqu | water | Aqueous |
| -ar, -ary | Adjective: resembling, related to | spectacular, unitary |
| arch | chief, first, rule | archangel, architect, archaic, monarchy, matriarchy, patriarchy, Archeozoic era |
| -ard, -art | Noun: characterized | braggart, drunkard, wizard |
| aster, astr | star | aster, asterisk, asteroid, astronomy, astronaut |
| -ate | Noun: state, office, function | candidate, electorate, delegate |
| -ate | Verb: cause to be | graduate, ameliorate, amputate, colligate |
| -ate | Adjective: kind of state | Inviolate |
| -ation | Noun: action, resulting state | specialization, aggravation, alternation |
| auc, aug, aut | to originate, to increase | augment, author, auction |
| aud, audi, aur, aus | to hear, listen | audience, audio, audible, auditorium, audiovisual, audition, auricular, auscultate |
| aug, auc | increase | augur, augment, auction |
| aut, auto | self | automobile, automatic, automotive, autograph, autonomous, autoimmune |
| bar | weight, pressure | Barometer |
| be | on, around, over, about, excessively, make, cause, name, affect | berate, bedeck, bespeak, belittle, beleaguer |
| belli | war | rebellion, belligerent, casus belli, bellicose |
| bene | good, well, gentle | benefactor, beneficial, benevolent, benediction, beneficiary, benefit |
| bi, bine | two | biped, bifurcate, biweekly, bivalve, biannual |
| bibl, bibli, biblio | book | bibliophile, bibliography, Bible |

| Root, Prefix or Suffix | Meaning | Examples |
|---|---|---|
| bio, bi | life | biography, biology, biometrics biome, biosphere |
| brev | short | abbreviate, brevity, brief |
| cad, cap, cas, ceiv, cept, capt, cid, cip | to take, to seize, to hold | receive, deceive, capable, capacious, captive, accident, capture, occasion, concept, intercept, forceps, except, reciprocate |
| cad, cas | to fall | cadaver, cadence, cascade |
| -cade | procession | motorcade |
| calor | heat | calorie, caloric, calorimeter |
| capit, capt | head | decapitate, capital, captain, caption |
| carn | flesh | carnivorous, incarnate, reincarnation, carnal |
| cat, cata, cath | down, with | catalogue, category, catheter |
| caus, caut | burn, heat | caustic, cauldron, cauterize |
| cause, cuse, cus | cause, motive | because, excuse, accusation |
| ceas, ced, cede, ceed, cess | to go, to yield, move, go, surrender | succeed, proceed, precede, recede, secession, exceed, succession |
| cent | hundred | centennial, century, centipede |
| centr, centri | center | eccentricity, centrifugal, concentric, eccentric |
| chrom | color | chrome, chromosome, polychrome, chromatic |
| chron | time | chronology, chronic, chronicle, chronometer, anachronism, synchronize |
| cide, cis, cise | to kill, to cut, cut down | fratricide, homicide, incision, circumcision, scissors |
| circum | around | circumnavigate, circumflex, circumstance, circumcision, circumference, circumorbital, circumlocution, circumvent, circumscribe, circulatory |
| cit | call, start | incite, citation, cite |

(*Continued*)

| Root, Prefix or Suffix | Meaning | Examples |
|---|---|---|
| civ | citizen | civic, civil, civilian, civilization |
| clam, claim | cry out | exclamation, clamor, proclamation, reclamation, acclaim |
| clin | lean, bend | decline, aclinic, inclination |
| clud, clus claus | to close, shut | include, exclude, clause, claustrophobia, enclose, exclusive, reclusive, conclude |
| co, cog, col, coll, con, com, cor | with, together | cohesiveness, cognate, collaborate, convene, commitment, compress, contemporary, converge, compact, confluence, convenient, concatenate, conjoin, combine, correct |
| cogn, gnos | to know | recognize, cognizant, diagnose, agnostic, incognito, prognosis |
| com, con | fully | complete, compel, conscious, condense, confess, confirm |
| contr, contra, counter | against, opposite | contradict, counteract, contravene, contrary, counterspy, contrapuntal |
| cord, cor, cardi | heart | cordial, concord, discord, courage, encourage |
| corp | body | corporation, corporal punishment, corpse, corpulent, corpus luteum |
| cort | correct | escort, cortege |
| cosm | universe, world | cosmos, microcosm, cosmopolitan, cosmonaut |
| cour, cur, curr, curs | run, course | occur, excursion, discourse, courier, course |
| crat, cracy | rule | autocrat, aristocrat, theocracy, technocracy |
| cre, cresc, cret, crease | grow | create, crescent, accretion, increase |
| crea | create | creature, recreation, creation |
| cred | believe | creed, credo, credence, credit, credulous, incredulous, incredible |

| Root, Prefix or Suffix | Meaning | Examples |
|---|---|---|
| cresc, cret, crease, cru | rise, grow | crescendo, concrete, increase, decrease, accrue |
| crit | separate, choose | critical, criterion, hypocrite |
| cur, curs | run | current, concurrent, concur, incur, recur, occur, courier, precursor, cursive |
| cura | care | curator, curative, manicure |
| cycl, cyclo | wheel, circle, circular | Cyclops, unicycle, bicycle, cyclone, cyclic |
| de- | from, down, away, to do the opposite, reverse, against | detach, deploy, derange, decrease, deodorize, devoid, deflate, degenerate |
| dec, deca | ten, ten times | decimal, decade, decalogue, decimate, decathlon |
| dec, dign | suitable | Decent, decorate, dignity |
| dei, div | God | divinity, divine, deity, divination, deify |
| dem, demo | people, populace, population | democracy, demography, demagogue, epidemic |
| dent, dont | tooth | dental, denture, orthodontist, periodontal |
| derm | skin, covering | hypodermic, dermatology, epidermis, taxidermy |
| di-, dy- | two, twice, double | divide, diverge, diglycerides |
| dia | through, across, between | diameter, diagonal, dialogue, dialect, dialectic, diagnosis, diachronic |
| dic, dict, dit | say, speak | dictation, dictionary, dictate, dictator, Dictaphone, edict, predict, verdict, contradict, benediction |
| dis, dif | not, opposite of, reverse, separate, deprive of, away | dismiss, differ, disallow, disperse, dissuade, divide, disconnect, disproportion, disrespect, distemper, disarray |
| dit | give | credit, audit |
| doc, doct | teach, prove | docile, doctor, doctrine, document, dogma, indoctrinate |

*(Continued)*

| Root, Prefix or Suffix | Meaning | Examples |
|---|---|---|
| domin | master, that which is under control | dominate, dominion, predominant, domain |
| don | give | donate, condone |
| dorm | sleep | dormant, dormitory |
| dox | thought, opinion, praise | orthodox, heterodox, paradox, doxology |
| -drome | run, step | syndrome, aerodrome, velodrome |
| duc, duct | to lead, pull | produce, abduct, product, transducer, viaduct, aqueduct, induct, deduct, reduce, induce |
| dura | hard, lasting | durable, duration, endure |
| dynam | power | dynamo, dynamic, dynamite, hydrodynamics |
| dys- | bad, abnormal, difficult, impaired, unfavorable | dysfunctional, dyslexia, dyspathy |
| e- | not, missing, out, fully, away, computer network related | emit, embed, eternal, ether, erase, email, e-tailer |
| ec- | out of, outside | echo, eclipse, eclectic, ecesis, ecstasy, eczema |
| eco- | household, environment, relating to ecology or economy | ecology, economize, ecospheres, ecomanagement |
| ecto- | outside, external | ectomorph, ectoderm, ectoplasm |
| -ed | Verb: past tense | dressed, faded, patted, closed, introduced |
| -ed | Adjective: having the quality or characteristics of | winged, moneyed, dogged, tiered |
| -en | Verb: to cause to become | lengthen, moisten, sharpen |
| -en | Adjective: material | golden, woolen, silken |
| en-, em- | put into, make, provide with, surround with | enamor, embolden, enslave, empower, entangle |
| -ence, -ency | Noun: action or process, quality or state | reference, emergency, dependence, eminence, latency |
| end- | inside, within | endorse, endocardial, endergonic, endoskeleton, endoscope, endogenous |

| Root, Prefix or Suffix | Meaning | Examples |
|---|---|---|
| epi- | upon, close to, over, after, altered | epicenter, epicarp, epilogue, epigone, epidiorite |
| equi- | equal | equidistant, equilateral, equilibrium, equinox, equation, equator |
| -er, -ier | Adjective: comparative | better, brighter, sooner, hotter, happier |
| -er, -or | Noun: person or thing that does something | flyer, reporter, player, member, fryer, collector, concentrator |
| -er, -or | Verb: action | ponder, dishonor, clamor |
| erg | work, effect | energy, erg, allergy, ergometer, ergograph, ergophobia |
| -ery | collective qualities, art, practice, trade, collection, state, condition | snobbery, bakery, greenery, gallery, slavery |
| -es, -ies | Noun: plural of most nouns ending in -ch, -s, -sh, -o and -z and some in -f and -y | passes, glasses, ladies, heroes |
| -es, -ies | Verb: third person singular present indicative of verbs that end in -ch, -s, -sh, - and some in -y | blesses, hushes, fizzes, defies |
| -ess | female | actress, goddess, poetess |
| -est, -iest | Adjective or Adverb: superlative | latest, strongest, luckiest, lyingest |
| ev-, et- | time, age | medieval, eternal |
| ex- | out of, away from, lacking, former | exit, exhale, exclusive, exceed, explosion, ex-mayor |
| exter-, extra-, extro- | outside of, beyond | external, extrinsic, extraordinary, extrapolate, extraneous, extrovert |
| fa, fess | speak | fable, fabulous, fame, famous, confess, profess |
| fac, fact, fec, fect, fic, fas, fea | do, make | difficult, fashion, feasible, feature, factory, fact, effect, manufacture, amplification, confection |
| fall, fals | deceive | fallacy, falsify, fallacious |
| femto | quadrillionth | femtosecond |
| fer | bear, carry | ferry, coniferous, fertile, defer, infer, refer, transfer |

*(Continued)*

| Root, Prefix or Suffix | Meaning | Examples |
|---|---|---|
| fic, feign, fain, fit, feat | shape, make, fashion | fiction, faint, feign |
| fid | belief, faith | confide, diffident, fidelity |
| fid, fide, feder | faith, trust | confidante, fidelity, confident, infidelity, infidel, federal, confederacy, semper fidelis |
| fig | shape, form | effigy, figure, figment |
| fila, fili | thread | filigree, filament, filter, filet, filibuster |
| fin | end, ended, finished | final, finite, finish, confine, fine, refine, define, finale |
| fix | repair, attach | fix, fixation, fixture, affix, prefix, suffix |
| flex, flect | bend | flex, reflex, flexible, flexor, inflexibility, reflect, deflect, circumflex |
| flict | strike | affliction, conflict, inflict |
| flu, fluc, fluv, flux | flow | influence, fluid, flue, flush, fluently, fluctuate, reflux, influx |
| -fold | Adverb: in a manner of, marked by | fourfold |
| for, fore | before | forecast, fortune, foresee |
| forc, fort | strength, strong | effort, fort, forte, fortifiable, fortify, fortitude |
| form | shape, resemble | form, format, conform, formulate, perform, formal, formula |
| fract, frag, frai | break | fracture, infraction, fragile, fraction, refract, frail |
| fuge | flee | subterfuge, refuge, centrifuge |
| -ful | Noun: an amount or quantity that fills | mouthful |
| -ful | Adjective: having, giving, marked by | fanciful |
| fuse | pour | confuse, transfuse |
| -fy | make, form into | falsify, dandify |
| gam | marriage | bigamy, monogamy, polygamy |
| gastr, gastro | stomach | gastric, gastronomic, gastritis, gastropod |

| Root, Prefix or Suffix | Meaning | Examples |
|---|---|---|
| gen | kind | generous |
| gen | birth, race, produce | genesis, genetics, eugenics, genealogy, generate, genetic, antigen, pathogen |
| geo | earth | geometry, geography, geocentric, geology |
| germ | vital part | germination, germ, germane |
| gest | carry, bear | congest, gestation |
| giga | billion | gigabyte, gigaflop |
| gin | careful | gingerly |
| gloss, glot | tongue | glossary, polyglot, epiglottis |
| glu, glo | lump, bond, glue | glue, agglutinate, conglomerate |
| gor | to gather, to bring together | category, categorize |
| grad, gress, gree | to gather, to bring together, step, go | grade, degree, progress, gradual, graduate, egress |
| graph, gram, graf | write, written, draw | graph, graphic, autograph, photography, graphite, telegram, polygraph, grammar, biography, lithograph |
| grat | pleasing | congratulate, gratuity, grateful, ingrate |
| grav | heavy, weighty | grave, gravity, aggravate, gravitate |
| greg | herd | gregarious, congregation, segregate, gregarian |
| hale, heal | make whole, sound | inhale, exhale, heal, healthy, healthiness |
| helio | sun | heliograph, heliotrope, heliocentric |
| hema, hemo | blood | hemorrhage, hemoglobin, hemophilia, hemostat |
| her, here, hes | stick | adhere, cohere, cohesion, inherent, hereditary, hesitate |
| hetero | other, different | heterodox, heterogeneous, heterosexual, heterodyne |
| hex, ses, sex | six | hexagon, hexameter, sestet, sextuplets |
| homo | same | homogenize, homosexual, homonym, homophone |

(*Continued*)

| Root, Prefix or Suffix | Meaning | Examples |
|---|---|---|
| hum, human | earth, ground, man | humus, exhume, humane |
| hydr, hydra, hydro | water | dehydrate, hydrant, hydraulic, hydraulics, hydrogen, hydrophobia |
| hyper | over, above | hyperactive, hypertensive, hyperbolic, hypersensitive, hyperventilate, hyperkinetic |
| hypn | sleep | hypnosis, hypnotherapy |
| -ia | Noun: names, diseases | phobia |
| -ian, an | Noun: related to, one that is | pedestrian, human |
| -iatry | Noun: art of healing | psychiatry |
| -ic | Adjective: quality, relation | generic |
| -ic, ics | Noun: related to the arts and sciences | arithmetic, economics |
| -ice | Noun: act | malice |
| -ify | Verb: cause | specify |
| ignis | fire | ignite, igneous, ignition |
| -ile | Adjective: having the qualities of | projectile |
| in, im | into, on, near, towards | instead, import |
| in, im, il, ir | not | illegible, irresolute, inaction, inviolate, innocuous, intractable, innocent, impregnable, impossible, imposter |
| infra | beneath | infrared, infrastructure |
| -ing | Noun: material made for, activity, result of an activity | flooring, swimming, building |
| -ing | Verb: present participle | depicting |
| -ing | Adjective: activity | cohering |
| inter | between, among | international, intercept, interject, intermission, internal, intermittent |
| intra | within, during, between layers, underneath | intramural, intranet, intranatal |
| intro | into, within, inward | interoffice, introvert, introspection, introduce |
| -ion | Noun: condition or action | abduction |
| -ish | Adjective: having the character of | newish |

| Root, Prefix or Suffix | Meaning | Examples |
|---|---|---|
| -ism | Noun: doctrine, belief, action or conduct | formalism |
| -ist | Noun: person or member | podiatrist |
| -ite | Noun: state or quality | graphite |
| -ity, ty | Noun: state or quality | lucidity, novelty |
| -ive | Noun: condition | native |
| -ive, -ative, -itive | Adjective: having the quality of | festive, cooperative, sensitive |
| -ize | Verb: cause | fantasize |
| jac, ject | throw | reject, eject, project, trajectory, interject, dejected, inject, ejaculate, adjacent |
| join, junct | join | adjoining, enjoin, juncture, conjunction, injunction |
| judice | judge | prejudice |
| jug, junct, just | to join | junction, adjust, conjugal |
| juven | young | juvenile, rejuvenate |
| labor | work | laborious, belabor |
| lau, lav, lot, lut | wash | launder, lavatory, lotion, ablution, dilute |
| lect, leg, lig | choose, gather, select, read | collect, legible, eligible |
| leg | law | legal, legislate, legislature, legitimize |
| -less | Adjective: without, missing | motiveless |
| levi | light | alleviate, levitate, levity |
| lex, leag, leg | law | legal, college, league |
| liber, liver | free | liberty, liberal, liberalize, deliverance |
| lide | strike | collide, nuclide |
| liter | letters | literary, literature, literal, alliteration, obliterate |
| loc, loco | place, area | location, locally, locality, allocate, locomotion |
| log, logo, ology | word, study, say, speech, reason, study | catalog, prologue, dialogue, zoology, logo |
| loqu, locut | talk, speak | eloquent, loquacious, colloquial, circumlocution |

(*Continued*)

| Root, Prefix or Suffix | Meaning | Examples |
|---|---|---|
| luc, lum, lun, lus, lust | light | translucent, luminary, luster, luna, illuminate, illustrate |
| lude | play | prelude |
| -ly | Adverb: in the manner of | fluently |
| macr-, macer | lean | emaciated, meager |
| magn | great | magnify, magnificent, magnanimous, magnate, magnitude, magnum |
| main | strength, foremost | mainstream, mainsail, domain, remain |
| mal | bad, badly | malformation, maladjusted, dismal, malady, malcontent, malfunction, malfeasance, maleficent |
| man, manu | hand, make, do | manual, manage, manufacture, manacle, manicure, manifest, maneuver, emancipate, management |
| mand | command | mandatory, remand, mandate |
| mania | madness | mania, maniac, kleptomania, pyromania |
| mar, mari, mer | sea, pool | marine, marsh, maritime, mermaid |
| matri | mother | matrimony, maternal, matriarchate, matron |
| medi | half, middle, between, halfway | mediate, medieval, Mediterranean, mediocre, medium |
| mega | great, million | megaphone, megaton, megaflop, megalomaniac, megabyte, megalopolis |
| mem | recall, remember | memo, commemoration, memento, memoir, memorable |
| ment | mind | mental, mention |
| -ment | Noun: condition or result | document |
| meso | middle | mesomorph, Mesoamerica, mesosphere |
| meta | beyond, change | metaphor, metamorphosis, metabolism, metahistorical, metainformation |

| Root, Prefix or Suffix | Meaning | Examples |
|---|---|---|
| meter | measure | meter, voltammeter, barometer, thermometer |
| metr | admeasure, apportion | metrics, asymmetric, parametric, telemetry |
| micro | small, millionth | microscope, microfilm, microcard, microwave, micrometer, microvolt |
| migra | wander | migrate, emigrant, immigrate |
| mill, kilo | thousand | millennium, kilobyte, kiloton |
| milli | thousandth | millisecond, milligram, millivolt |
| min | little, small | minute, minor, minuscule |
| mis | wrong, bad, badly | misconduct, misinform, misinterpret, mispronounce, misnomer, mistake, misogynist |
| mit, miss | send | emit, remit, submit, admit, commit, permit, transmit, omit, intermittent, mission, missile |
| mob, mov, mot | move | motion, remove, mobile, motor |
| mon | warn, remind | monument, admonition, monitor, premonition |
| mono | one | monopoly, monotype, monologue, mononucleosis, monorail, monotheist |
| mor, mort | mortal, death | mortal, immortal, mortality, mortician, mortuary |
| morph | shape, form | amorphous, dimorphic, metamorphosis, morphology, polymorphic, morpheme, amorphous |
| multi | many, much | multifold, multilingual, multiped, multiply, multitude, multipurpose, multinational |
| nano | billionth | nanosecond, nanobucks |
| nasc, nat, gnant, nai | to be born | nascent, native, pregnant, naive |
| nat, nasc | to be from, to spring forth | innate, natal, native, renaissance |
| neo | new | Neolithic, nouveau riche, neologism, neophyte, neonate |

(*Continued*)

| Root, Prefix or Suffix | Meaning | Examples |
|---|---|---|
| -ness | Noun: state, condition, quality | kindness |
| neur | nerve | neuritis, neuropathic, neurologist, neural, neurotic |
| nom | law, order | autonomy, astronomy, gastronomy, economy |
| nom, nym | name | nominate, synonym |
| nomen, nomin | name | nomenclature, nominate, ignominious |
| non | nine | nonagon |
| non | not | nonferrous, nonsense, nonabrasive, nondescript |
| nov | new | novel, renovate, novice, nova, innovate |
| nox, noc | night | nocturnal, equinox, noctilucent |
| numer | number | numeral, numeration, enumerate, innumerable |
| numisma | coin | numismatics |
| ob, oc, of, op | toward, against, in the way | oppose, occur, offer, obtain |
| oct | eight | octopus, octagon, octogenarian, octave |
| oligo | few, little | Oligocene, oligosaccharide, oligotrophic, oligarchy |
| omni | all, every | omnipotent, omniscient, omnipresent, omnivorous |
| onym | name | anonymous, pseudonym, antonym, synonym |
| oper | work | operate, cooperate, opus |
| -or | Noun: condition or activity | valor, honor, humor, minor |
| ortho | straight, correct | orthodox, orthodontist, orthopedic, unorthodox |
| -ory | Noun: place for, serves for | territory, rectory |
| -ous, -eous, -ose, -ious | Adjective: having the quality of, relating to | adventurous, courageous, verbose, fractious |
| over | excessive, above | overwork, overall |
| pac | peace | pacifist, pacify, Pacific ocean |
| pair, pare | arrange, assemblage, two | repair, impair, compare, prepare |

| Root, Prefix or Suffix | Meaning | Examples |
|---|---|---|
| paleo | old | Paleozoic, Paleolithic, paleomagnetism, paleopsychology |
| pan | all | Pan-American, pan-African, panacea, pandemonium (place of all the demons) |
| para | beside | paradox, paraprofessional, paramedic, paraphrase, parachute |
| pat, pass, path | feel, suffer | patient, passion, sympathy, pathology |
| pater, patr | father | paternity, patriarch, patriot, patron, patronize |
| path, pathy | feeling, suffering | pathos, sympathy, antipathy, apathy, telepathy |
| ped, pod | foot | pedal, impede, pedestrian, centipede, tripod, podiatry, antipode, podium |
| pedo | child | orthopedic, pedagogue, pediatrics |
| pel, puls | drive, push, urge | compel, dispel, expel, repel, propel, pulse, impulse, pulsate, compulsory, expulsion, repulsive |
| pend, pens, pond | hang, weigh | pendant, pendulum, suspend, appendage, pensive, append |
| per | through, intensive | persecute, permit, perspire, perforate, persuade |
| peri | around | periscope, perimeter, perigee, periodontal |
| phage | eat | macrophage, bacteriophage |
| phan, phas, phen, fan, phant, fant | show, make visible | phantom, fantasy |
| phe | speak | blaspheme, cipher, phenomenon, philosopher |
| phil | love | philosopher, philanthropy, philharmonic, bibliophile |
| phlegma | inflammation | phlegm, phlegmatic |

(*Continued*)

| Root, Prefix or Suffix | Meaning | Examples |
|---|---|---|
| phobia, phobos | fear | phobia, claustrophobia, acrophobia, aquaphobia, ergophobia, homophobia |
| phon | sound | telephone, phonics, phonograph, phonetic, homophone, microphone, symphony, euphonious |
| phot, photo | light | photograph, photoelectric, photogenic, photosynthesis, photon |
| pico | trillionth | picofarad, picocurie, picovolt |
| pict | paint, show, draw | picture, depict |
| plac, plais | please | placid, placebo, placate, complacent |
| pli, ply | fold | reply, implicate, ply |
| plore | cry out, wail | implore, exploration, deploring |
| plu, plur, plus | more | plural, pluralist, plus |
| pneuma, pneumon | breath | pneumatic, pneumonia |
| pod | foot, feet | podiatry, tripod |
| poli | city | metropolis, police, politics, Indianapolis, megalopolis, acropolis |
| poly | many | polytheist, polygon, polygamy, polymorphous |
| pon, pos, pound | place, put | postpone, component, opponent, proponent, expose, impose, deposit, posture, position, expound, impound |
| pop | people | population, populous, popular |
| port | carry | porter, portable, transport, report, export, import, support, transportation |
| portion | part, share | portion, proportion |
| post | after, behind | postpone, postdate |
| pot | power | potential, potentate, impotent |
| pre, pur | before | precede |

| Root, Prefix or Suffix | Meaning | Examples |
|---|---|---|
| prehendere | seize, grasp | apprehend, comprehend, comprehensive, prehensile |
| prin, prim, prime | first | primacy, prima donna, primitive, primary, primal, primeval, prince, principal |
| pro | for, forward | propel |
| proto | first | prototype, protocol, protagonist, protozoan, Proterozoic, protoindustrial |
| psych | mind, soul | psyche, psychiatry, psychology, psychosis |
| punct | point, dot | punctual, punctuation, puncture, acupuncture |
| pute | think | dispute, computer |
| quat, quad | four | quadrangle, quadruplets |
| quint, penta | five | quintet, quintuplets, pentagon, pentane, pentameter |
| quip | ship | equip, equipment |
| quir, quis, quest, quer | seek, ask | query, inquire, exquisite, quest |
| re | back, again | report, realign, retract, revise, regain |
| reg, recti | straighten | regiment, regular, rectify, correct, direct, rectangle |
| retro | backwards | retrorocket, retrospect, retrogression, retroactive |
| ri, ridi, risi | laughter | deride, ridicule, ridiculous, derision, risible |
| rog, roga | ask | prerogative, interrogation, derogatory |
| rupt | break | rupture, interrupt, abrupt, disrupt, ruptible |
| sacr, sanc, secr | sacred | sacred, sacrosanct, sanction, consecrate, desecrate |
| salv, salu | safe, healthy | salvation, salvage, salutation |
| sanct | holy | sanctify, sanctuary, sanction, sanctimonious, sacrosanct |
| sat, satis | enough | satient, saturate, satisfy |

(*Continued*)

| Root, Prefix or Suffix | Meaning | Examples |
|---|---|---|
| sci, scio, scientia | know | science, conscious, omniscient, cognoscenti |
| scope | see, watch | telescope, microscope, kaleidoscope, periscope, stethoscope |
| scrib, script | write | scribe, scribble, inscribe, describe, subscribe, prescribe, manuscript |
| se | apart, move away from | secede |
| sect, sec | cut | intersect, transect, dissect, secant, section |
| sed, sess, sid | sit | sediment, session, obsession, possess, preside, president, reside, subside |
| semi | half, partial | semifinal, semiconscious, semiannual, semimonthly, semicircle |
| sen, scen | old, grow old | senior, senator, senile, senescence, evanescent |
| sent, sens | feel, think | sentiment, consent, resent, dissent, sentimental, sense, sensation, sensitive, sensory, dissension |
| sept | seven | septet, septennial |
| sequ, secu, sue | follow | sequence, consequence, sequel, subsequent, prosecute, consecutive, second, ensue, pursue |
| serv | save, serve, keep | servant, service, subservient, servitude, preserve, conserve, reservation, deserve, conservation, observe |
| -ship | Noun: status, condition | relationship, friendship |
| sign, signi | sign, mark, seal | signal, signature, design, insignia, significant |
| simil, simul | like, resembling | similar, assimilate, simulate, simulacrum, simultaneous |
| sist, sta, stit | stand, withstand, make up | assist, insist, persist, circumstance, stamina, status, state, static, stable, stationary, substitute |
| soci | to join, companions | sociable, society |

| Root, Prefix or Suffix | Meaning | Examples |
|---|---|---|
| sol, solus | alone | solo, soliloquy, solitaire, solitude, solitary, isolate |
| solv, solu, solut | loosen, explain | solvent, solve, absolve, resolve, soluble, solution, resolution, resolute, dissolute, absolution |
| somn | sleep | insomnia, somnambulist |
| soph | wise | sophomore (wise fool), philosophy, sophisticated |
| spec, spect, spi, spic | look, see | specimen, specific, spectator, spectacle, aspect, speculate, inspect, respect, prospect, retrospective, introspective, expect, conspicuous |
| sper | render favorable | prosper |
| sphere | ball, sphere | sphere, stratosphere, hemisphere, spheroid |
| spir | breath | spirit, conspire, inspire, aspire, expire, perspire, respiration |
| stand, stant, stab, stat, stan, sti, sta, st, stead | stand | stature, establish, stance |
| -ster | person | mobster, monster |
| strain, strict, string, stige | bind, pull, draw tight | stringent, strict, restrict, constrict, restrain, boa constrictor |
| stru, struct, stroy, stry | build | construe, structure, construct, instruct, obstruct, destruction, destroy, industry, ministry |
| sub, suc, suf, sup, sur, sus | under, below, from, secretly, instead of | sustain, survive, support, suffice, succeed, submerge, submarine, substandard, subnormal, subvert |
| sume, sump | take, use, waste | consume, assume, sump, presumption |
| super, supra | over, above | superior, suprarenal, superscript, supernatural, superimpose, supercede |
| syn, sym | together, at the same time | sympathy, synthesis, synchronous, syndicate |

(*Continued*)

| Root, Prefix or Suffix | Meaning | Examples |
|---|---|---|
| tact, tang, tag, tig, ting | touch | tactile, contact, intact, intangible, tangible, contagious, contiguous, contingent |
| tain, ten, tent, tin | hold, keep, have | retain, continue, content, tenacious |
| tect, teg | cover | detect, protect, tegular, tegument |
| tele | distance, far, from afar | telephone, telegraph, telegram, telescope, television, telephoto, telecast, telepathy |
| tem, tempo | time | tempo, temporary, extemporaneously, contemporary, pro tem, temporal |
| ten, tin, tain | hold | tenacious, tenant, tenure, untenable, detention, retentive, content, pertinent, continent, obstinate, contain, abstain, pertain, detain |
| tend, tent, tens | stretch, strain | tendency, extend, intend, contend, pretend, superintend, tender, extent, tension, pretense |
| tera | trillion | terabyte, teraflop |
| term | end, boundary, limit | exterminate, terminal |
| terr, terra | earth | terrain, terrarium, territory, terrestrial |
| test | to bear witness | testament, detest, testimony, attest, testify |
| the, theo | God, a god | monotheism, polytheism, atheism, theology |
| therm | heat | thermometer, theorem, thermal, thermos bottle, thermostat, hypothermia |
| thesis, thet | place, put | antithesis, hypothesis, synthesis, epithet |
| tire | draw, pull | attire, retire, entire |
| tom | cut | atom (not cuttable), appendectomy, tonsillectomy, dichotomy, anatomy |
| tor, tors, tort | twist | torture, retort, extort, distort, contort, torsion, tortuous, torturous |

| Root, Prefix or Suffix | Meaning | Examples |
|---|---|---|
| tox | poison | toxic, intoxicate, antitoxin |
| tract, tra, trai, treat | drag, draw, pull | attract, tractor, traction, extract, retract, protract, detract, subtract, contract, intractable |
| trans | across, beyond, change | transform, transoceanic, transmit, transportation, transducer |
| tri | three | tripod, triangle, trinity, trilateral |
| trib | pay, bestow | tribute, contribute, attribute, retribution, tributary |
| tribute | give | contribute, distribute, tributary |
| turbo | disturb | turbulent, disturb, turbid, turmoil |
| typ | print | type, prototype, typical, typography, typewriter, typology, typify |
| ultima | last | ultimate, ultimatum |
| umber, umbraticum | shadow | umbra, penumbra, (take) umbrage, adumbrate |
| un | not, against, opposite | unceasing, unequal |
| uni | one | uniform, unilateral, universal, unity, unanimous, unite, unison, unicorn |
| -ure | Noun: act, condition, process, function | exposure, conjecture, measure |
| vac | empty | vacate, vacuum, evacuate, vacation, vacant, vacuous |
| vade | go | evade, invader |
| vale, vali, valu | strength, worth | equivalent, valiant, validity, evaluate, value, valor |
| veh, vect | to carry | vector, vehicle, convection, vehement |
| ven, vent | come | convene, intervene, venue, convenient, avenue, circumvent, invent, convent, venture, event, advent, prevent |
| ver, veri | true | very, aver, verdict, verity, verify, verisimilitude |
| verb, verv | word | verify, veracity, verbalize, verve |

(*Continued*)

| Root, Prefix or Suffix | Meaning | Examples |
|---|---|---|
| vert, vers | turn, change | convert, revert, advertise, versatile, vertigo, invert, reversion, extravert, introvert, diversion, introvert, convertible, reverse, controversy |
| vi | way | viable, vibrate, vibrant |
| vic, vicis | change, substitute | vicarious, vicar, vicissitude |
| vict, vinc | conquer | victor, evict, convict, convince, invincible |
| vid, vis | see | video, evident, provide, providence, visible, revise, supervise, vista, visit, vision, review, indivisible |
| viv, vita, vivi | alive, life | revive, survive, vivid, vivacious, vitality, vivisection, vital, vitamins, revitalize |
| voc, voke | call | vocation, avocation, convocation, invocation, evoke, provoke, revoke, advocate, provocative, vocal |
| vol | will | malevolent, benevolent, volunteer, volition |
| volcan | fire | volcano, vulcanize, Vulcan |
| volv, volt, vol | turn about, roll | revolve, voluble, voluminous, convolution, revolt, evolution |
| vor | eat greedily | voracious, carnivorous, herbivorous, omnivorous, devour |
| -ward | Adverb: in a direction or manner | homeward |
| -wise | Adverb: in the manner of, with regard to | timewise, clockwise, bitwise |
| with | against | withhold, without, withdraw, forthwith |
| -y | Noun: state, condition, result of an activity | society, victory |
| -y | Adjective: marked by, having | hungry, angry, smeary, teary |
| zo | animal | zoo (zoological garden), zoology, zodiac, protozoan |

| Root/Prefix/Suffix | Words Found in Course Texts | Meanings of the Words |
|---|---|---|
| | | |
| | | |
| | | |
| | | |
| | | |

## Context Clues

The words surrounding an unknown word often give you an idea of what the word might mean. These hints and suggestions come in four main types of clues: example, logic, definition, and contrast.

| | Definition | Signal Words | Illustration |
|---|---|---|---|
| **Logic** | Sentence sense reveals meaning of the word | No signal words because the sentence meanings reveals the word meaning | From a window, one could tell **precipitation** was in the forecast because everyone carried an umbrella (umbrella indicates rain). |
| **Definition** | When the writer provides the meaning of the word in the sentence | That is, or, also known as, to define as, namely, in other words, which means | The **demagogue**, also **known as** a leader who incites action in people, appealed to the crowds emotions. |

*(Continued)*

| | Definition | Signal Words | Illustration |
|---|---|---|---|
| **Example** | An example or illustration is offered in the sentence revealing the meaning of the word | For example, for instance, to illustrate, as in the case, as represented, as shown, like | A **democracy, as represented** in the United States, is being chosen by more countries for a form of government. |
| **Contrast** | Indicates meaning of a word by showing the opposite | But, however, in contrast, whereas, on the other hand, on the contrary, even though, yet, instead, although | The report gave **credence** to the argument, **whereas** the committee's reaction was complete **disbelief**. |

## Activity Three: Recognizing Context Clues

While reading for your courses, identify the following context clues to identify the meanings of unknown words. Keep track of the words and context clues in the chart below.

| Unknown Word | Type of Context Clue (Logic, Example, Definition, Contrast) | Signal Words | Meaning of Word |
|---|---|---|---|
| | | | |
| | | | |
| | | | |
| | | | |

## Activity Four: Plan for Using New Words

Make a conscious effort to use three of the new words you have listed in the charts for this week. Use the chart below to keep track of when and how you used the words. What reactions did you receive from others when you used the new words?

| New Word Used | When Did You Use the Word? Example. | How/Context in Which You Used the Word? | What Reaction Did You Receive When You Used the Word? |
|---|---|---|---|
| | | | |
| | | | |
| | | | |

**Weekly Goals** **Week of:** ______________________

**What am I grateful for?**

**What are your goal(s) for the week?**

| **Course:** | ______ | ______ | ______ | ______ | ______ | ______ |
|---|---|---|---|---|---|---|
| • To do: | | | | | | |
| • Strateg(ies): | | | | | | |
| • Resource(s): | | | | | | |

**Personal Wellness/Spirituality:**

**Family & Friends:**

## Weekly Planner

**Week of:** ______________________

| | Monday | Tuesday | Wednesday | Thursday | Friday | Saturday | Sunday |
|---|---|---|---|---|---|---|---|
| 06:00 am | | | | | | | |
| 06:30 am | | | | | | | |
| 07:00 am | | | | | | | |
| 07:30 am | | | | | | | |
| 08:00 am | | | | | | | |
| 08:30 am | | | | | | | |
| 09:00 am | | | | | | | |
| 09:30 am | | | | | | | |
| 10:00 am | | | | | | | |
| 10:30 am | | | | | | | |
| 11:00 am | | | | | | | |
| 11:30 am | | | | | | | |
| 12:00 pm | | | | | | | |
| 12:30 pm | | | | | | | |
| 01:00 pm | | | | | | | |
| 01:30 pm | | | | | | | |
| 02:00 pm | | | | | | | |
| 02:30 pm | | | | | | | |
| 03:00 pm | | | | | | | |
| 03:30 pm | | | | | | | |
| 04:00 pm | | | | | | | |
| 04:30 pm | | | | | | | |
| 05:00 pm | | | | | | | |
| 05:30 pm | | | | | | | |
| 06:00 pm | | | | | | | |
| 06:30 pm | | | | | | | |
| 07:00 pm | | | | | | | |
| 07:30 pm | | | | | | | |
| 08:00 pm | | | | | | | |
| 08:30 pm | | | | | | | |
| 09:00 pm | | | | | | | |
| 09:30 pm | | | | | | | |
| 10:00 pm | | | | | | | |
| 10:30 pm | | | | | | | |

## Important Thoughts / Things to Remember / Doodling

# Week Seven

# Annotating with Critical Thinking & Reading Strategies

While the active reading strategies introduced in Week Five, such as SQ3R and THIEVES, are very effective with textbook reading, they are not going to work for all reading assignments. This will especially be true with assignments that require close, careful, and critical reading. In these types of assignments, you will likely need to use the strategies of inquiry that require exploration, reflection, evaluation, and analysis. For this type of reading, you will need to annotate while asking the text questions that involve close critical thinking and critical reading skills. This week's activities will engage you in using the tools necessary for this type of close and careful critical reading. The activities will also challenge you to identify assignments where this type of reading is necessary and to apply the strategies to some of your existing assignments.

## Rhetorical Analysis

Critical reading and thinking critically about a text requires that you engage in a process called rhetorical analysis. This process considers audience, purpose, and context (situation). While you read, you engage in a conversation with the text. You question it, share your observations with it, agree with it, disagree with it, note your observations, and connect with it. All of this conversing occurs through annotating and marking on the text. And, rhetorical analysis guides you in the process.

Rhetorical analysis

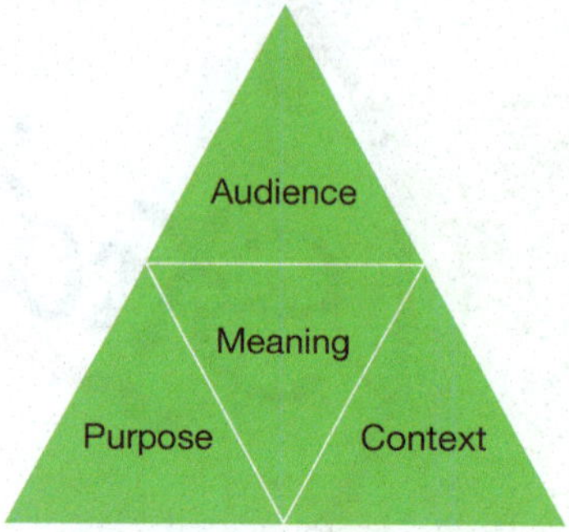


- Who is the audience?
- What is the purpose?
- What is the context (situation of writing/or genre being written in)?

## Activity One: Active Reading

Choose a reading assignment for one of your courses. While you read, ask the text the following questions and note your observations and responses to the questions by annotating the text.

### Audience

- Who was the text written for? What assumptions did the author make about his or her audience when he or she was writing the text? How do you know? What in the text reveals this?
- What assumptions did your professor make about you as an audience in assigning the reading? How are you a different or similar audience than the audience the text was written for?

### Purpose

- Why did the author write the text? What was his or her purpose for writing? How do you know? Was the purpose achieved? Why or why not? What in the text supports this?
- Why did your professor assign this reading as part of the course? How does it fit in with the learning outcomes of the course? What should you take away from this reading?

### Context (Situation)

- What was the context (situation) that the text was written? In other words, what genre (textbook, persuasive essay, informative essay, short story, play, novel, newspaper article, magazine article, peer-reviewed journal article, editorial) was it written in? What time period? How did this affect the style, diction, and organization of the text? What are the expectations of this context? Is it a reliable and truthful text? How does the text fit within the context of the course? How does this affect meaning? How should it be read and considered?

## Conversing with a Text

Thinking of reading as a conversation can change the way that you read forever. It can mean that you will never be able to read without a pen or pencil in hand again! This will also ensure that your reading will stay active. When you are actively conversing with another person, you are not only listening to that person with full attention but also responding back to that person. In responding you are summarizing and clarifying important points—"What I hear you saying is…;" Disagreeing or agreeing—"I don't agree with that perspective;" Questioning—"I am not sure I understand what that means;" Connecting and reflecting—"Hmmm. That reminds me of time when…I wonder if…;" and Evaluating—"That is an overgeneralization and really needs further support."

Critical reading entails this same type of active and lively dialogue. However, to converse with a text you need to mark this lively exchange with a pen or pencil. Some students like to highlight. However, it is hard to have this type of conversation with a highlighter. Thus, a highlighter is still a somewhat passive activity. And, unless it is strategically coded and done after a conversation has occurred as described above, it is not very useful. When looking back at highlighted text, it is often hard to remember why it was highlighted. However, written notes and annotations reveal exactly what you were thinking while you read the text. They serve as a transcription of the conversation. And, you can add to it with a different color of pen—allowing you to track the different conversations you had with each reading.

## Activity Two: Have a Conversation

Choose a reading assignment from one of your classes where you need to read closely in order to reflect, respond, analyze, and/or evaluate the reading. While you read, use rhetorical analysis to note the main ideas of the reading. Also, mark your observations, reactions, and connections in the margins. Then, after you read, respond to the following questions to have a deeper conversation with the text.

- What I hear you saying is:
  (Summarize the main points of the essay)
  ________________________________________________
  ________________________________________________
  ________________________________________________
- I agree with you when you say ______________ because it reminds me of ______________.
- I disagree with you when you say ______________ because ______________.
- I do not understand what you mean when you say ______________. Please tell me more about ______________.
- ______________ says ______________, which leads me to believe that you and he agree about ______________. However, I wonder if you might disagree about ______________. I would like to hear both of you talk about ______________.
- I can apply what you are saying to ______________ because ______________.

## Activity Three: Active Annotating: OCD Reading

1. Choose an article from one of your classes that you need to read critically.
2. Annotate the article with the OCD strategy. Note **O**bservations (concepts and ideas in the article that relate to class material), **C**onnections (places in the article that relate to you and your life, deepen your understanding of life events), **D**iscussion (questions that are brought up for you to talk about in class, questions you now want to research deeper, anything you don't understand or have a deeper curiosity about). Underline the section and write the letter next to it. Add brief notes that will help you remember what you were thinking.

### OBSERVE, CONNECT, DISCUSS

- As you read, use the strategy OCD to actively mark while you read

- **Observe** and note key ideas that are related to course objectives and outcomes that might be on the test. (Syllabus, course notes, power points, and end of chapter questions can help you identify this before reading.)
- **Connect** and note in the margins when the reading relates to your own experiences.
- **Discuss**—note questions for your professor and classmates. So, you are prepared to discuss the material in class.

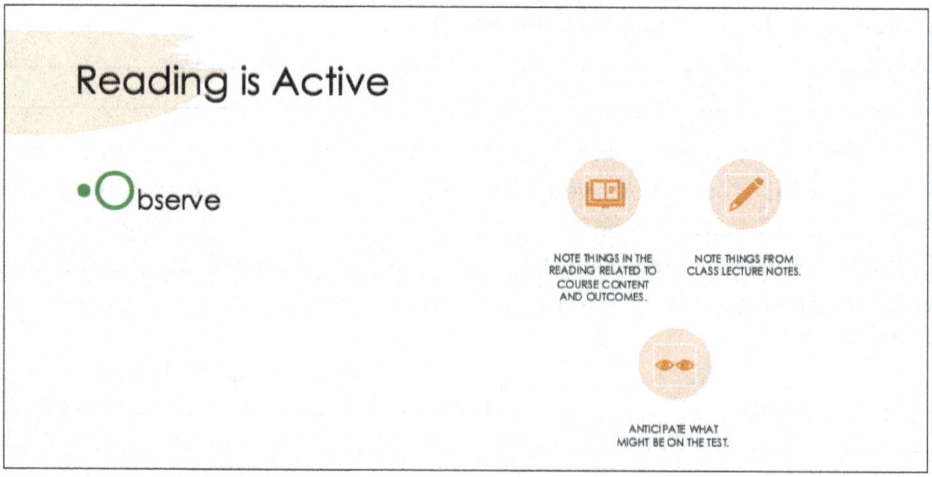

## Reading poses questions

- **D**iscuss

Note things that you don't understand to ask your professor.

Note big questions that you want to talk about in class with your professor and classmates.

## Reading relates

- **C**onnect

Ask yourself and note how the material relates to you and your experiences?

Make connections to current events.

Relate and note how the material connects to your career goals.

Connect the reading to your other courses.

## Activity Four: Using a Reading Journal with OCD

The reading journal allows you to reflect on and report on your active interaction with a text. **It is your space for actively questioning, reacting to, and connecting with the meaning and messages** of the texts you are reading and annotating. It will not only give you a chance to reflect upon and synthesize your reactions to the readings but also give you are an organizational strategy for writing and reading assignments—to deepen your understanding and of the texts and improve your writing about the texts. A reading journal can be especially helpful for the pre-writing stages of a paper, creating an annotated bibliography for research papers, keeping track of your research for a paper, and improving class discussion and understanding of course material.

### Process

1. **While you read . . .**

   Use the same method you used in Activity Three while reading a text assigned for class—noting **Observations, Connections, Discussion Questions**. You should be having a conversation with the author. As mentioned previously, during your interaction with the text, you should think about and note how the information relates to your own experiences, might be adapted and used in your courses, and compares and contrasts with what you have learned in class and from other texts you read.

2. **After you read and annotate. . .**

   After you read, you should look at your annotations and reflect on them and organize them in a Reading Journal. (Use the following template).

   Your reading journal is a Word document that you add to each week. Here you should:

   - List the article/text you read in APA or MLA reference style (See Purdue OWL or the APA/MLA style handbook https://owl.purdue.edu/owl/research_and_citation/resources.html).
   - Note Observations, Connections, Discussion Questions. Record your ***interaction with the text*** that you had while you read. Include the textual reference and page number with your interaction/what you thought or the question you had about it—how you connected or how you will apply it and use it. Entries need not be long (sentence or two).
   - Save the template and use it for your classes to improve reading comprehension, class participation and performance on writing assignments.

| **Article (APA or MLA format)** | **Observations** (include page #)<br><br>(Concepts related to class or other articles/readings.) | **Connections** (include page #)<br><br>(Relates to your life experiences/life events. Connects to other classes.) | **Discussion Questions** (include page #)<br><br>(What interesting questions might you discuss in class? Research further? What don't you understand?) | **Ideas for Presentation/ Class paper/ assignment**<br><br>(How will you use this in your paper/ assignment?) |
|---|---|---|---|---|
| | | | | |
| | | | | |
| | | | | |
| | | | | |
| | | | | |
| | | | | |
| | | | | |

**Weekly Goals** **Week of:** ____________________

**What am I grateful for?**

**What are your goal(s) for the week?**

| **Course:** | ________ | ________ | ________ | ________ | ________ | ________ |
|---|---|---|---|---|---|---|
| • To do: | | | | | | |
| • Strateg(ies): | | | | | | |
| • Resource(s): | | | | | | |

**Personal Wellness/Spirituality:**

**Family & Friends:**

**Weekly Planner** **Week of:** ____________________

| | Monday | Tuesday | Wednesday | Thursday | Friday | Saturday | Sunday |
|---|---|---|---|---|---|---|---|
| 06:00 am | | | | | | | |
| 06:30 am | | | | | | | |
| 07:00 am | | | | | | | |
| 07:30 am | | | | | | | |
| 08:00 am | | | | | | | |
| 08:30 am | | | | | | | |
| 09:00 am | | | | | | | |
| 09:30 am | | | | | | | |
| 10:00 am | | | | | | | |
| 10:30 am | | | | | | | |
| 11:00 am | | | | | | | |
| 11:30 am | | | | | | | |
| 12:00 pm | | | | | | | |
| 12:30 pm | | | | | | | |
| 01:00 pm | | | | | | | |
| 01:30 pm | | | | | | | |
| 02:00 pm | | | | | | | |
| 02:30 pm | | | | | | | |
| 03:00 pm | | | | | | | |
| 03:30 pm | | | | | | | |
| 04:00 pm | | | | | | | |
| 04:30 pm | | | | | | | |
| 05:00 pm | | | | | | | |
| 05:30 pm | | | | | | | |
| 06:00 pm | | | | | | | |
| 06:30 pm | | | | | | | |
| 07:00 pm | | | | | | | |
| 07:30 pm | | | | | | | |
| 08:00 pm | | | | | | | |
| 08:30 pm | | | | | | | |
| 09:00 pm | | | | | | | |
| 09:30 pm | | | | | | | |
| 10:00 pm | | | | | | | |
| 10:30 pm | | | | | | | |

## Important Thoughts / Things to Remember / Doodling

## Week Eight

# Studying and Learning in College

By this point in the semester, you have likely had at least one test and have experienced some studying and testing in college. Many students find college to be much different than high school. You might also be finding this to be the case. The study strategies (sometimes nonexistent) that worked in high school may not be working for you in college.

It is not uncommon for students to come to my office in frustration and tears looking for direction for studying in college. They often explain that they studied for 6 or more hours and still failed the test. Frustrated and overwhelmed, many feel that they are not smart enough for college.

At this point, I ask them to describe how they study. In almost all cases, I hear something like this: "I review my notes and make flash cards." When I ask what their flashcards consist of, they tell me: "The word on the front—and definition on the back."

The problem with this study method is that it is passive and doesn't activate memory and learning strategies that involve meaning. Meaning is essential for moving the information from short-term memory to long-term memory. Students also need to realize that college learning requires learning material on higher levels than the knowledge (memorization) level of learning. Next week, we go over strategies for learning material on all levels of learning with Bloom's Taxonomy. But, first—you need to understand how memory works.

## Memory

For information to be learned and remembered, it must move through a process where it is encoded, stored, and retrieved. You encode information and place it in your short-term memory when you attach meaning to it; you then store information in your long-term memory and retrieve it when you organize it through effective study processes. Thus, you can see where simply looking over notes or creating flashcards where you write textbook definitions would not move information from short-term memory into long-term memory. Looking over the notes does not really attach any new meaning to the notes, and it does not require you to store or retrieve the information. Thus, the information never moves into long-term memory. When the students were taking the test, they couldn't retrieve the information because it was never stored. Additionally, creating flashcards where you memorize definitions without attaching your own meaning to the information never moves the new information beyond your short-term memory because you have not given new meaning and understanding to the information. Thus, it never moves beyond your short-term memory (Bourne, Dominowski, and Healy, 1986).

Students who studied in high school with short-term memory devices such as flash cards may have found some success if the test questions were testing knowledge learning only and if the students had crammed the night before. The information likely remained in the short-term memory long enough to succeed in the test the next day. However, students likely are unable to recall any of that information now. Why? The information never moved to the long-term memory.

To encode meaning to this concept of memory, you might think of how memory and storage work on a computer. If you open a Word document and type information into it but do not save it, what happens when you go to look for it later? It is gone. The computer never saved it because you never attached any meaningful path for it to remember it in memory—and thus it could not retrieve it from its long-term memory because it was never placed there. However, if you attach a name to it and store it in a meaningful place (such as a folder devoted to your class), you can retrieve it later. To extend this example further, the more organized the pathway you create for saving the document, the easier it will be to retrieve it later. For example, if you don't give it a meaningful name, it may be on the computer somewhere, but it may take a very long time to remember where you stored it. Finding it may be complicated. However, if you save it in an organized manner, give it a name related to

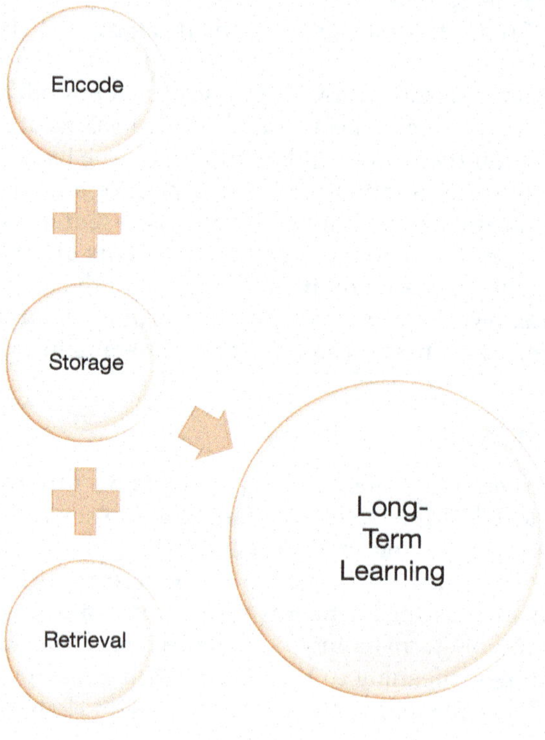

the document, create a folder for the course, and save it in the course folder, you will easily be able to find where it is later.

This is also true when you study. If your studying attaches meaning in organized ways, you will be able to retrieve the information easily during the test, and the information will remain in your long-term memory beyond the day of the test.

So, how do you develop more effective and organized methods of studying?

One method that students find success with is the use of concept cards. Since many students used flash cards in high school, they find this method easily adaptable to their previous methods. And it promotes moving information from short-term memory to long-term memory.

## Concept Cards

Concept cards are different than flash cards because they help you to encode meaning, store the new meaning and attached information in an organized fashion, and give you a retrieval system that allows you multiple, organized pathways.

The following five activities take you through the steps for creating concept cards for one of your classes. You can then use the same process for your other courses where it might be appropriate for learning and studying new terms and concepts.

## Activity One: Using Word in Sentences

Choose a course where it is important to learn many new terms and concepts. Use the syllabus, textbook, and class notes to identify which terms you will need to know for the test. Make a list of the terms or concepts.

On the front of an index card write the new word or concept. Below the word, use the word in an applied sentence and embed context clues (see chart from Week Six) so that the sentence reveals the meaning of the word. The sentence should not be a definition sentence. By using the word in a sentence, you are beginning encoding and creating learning on the level of application. Many test questions ask that you APPLY meaning. Next week, you will learn that this is one of the higher levels of learning of Bloom's Taxonomy that are used for writing test questions. In order to find success in college you will need to learn and study material on all levels of Bloom's Taxonomy. Just writing this sentence begins this level of learning and begins to store the new material in your long-term memory. See Figure 8.1.

**Figure 8.1: Front Side of a Concept Card. Quantitative Research Methods**

The sociology professor used **quantitative research** methods when he interpreted the **survey data using SPSS software and created a table** showing that more men than women return to college to finish a degree after leaving.

## Activity Two: In Your Own Words

On the back of the index cards, divide the card into four squares. In the first two squares, define the word. BUT—go beyond the definition of the textbook. In the first box, write the textbook definition, and in the second box (beside it), paraphrase the definition into YOUR OWN WORDS. This further establishes the encoding that began on the front of the card by attaching meaning.

**Figure 8.2: Backside View of Concept Card Boxes One and Two**

| | |
|---|---|
| Quantitative methods use objective measurements and numerical analysis of data collected through polls, questionnaires or surveys (Babbie, 2010) | Quantitate methods believe that objective data can be gathered and analyzed through processes such as surveys, polls, and questionnaires—emphasis is placed on numbers and measurements |
| | |

## Activity Three: Creating Visual Images

Another powerful encoding technique is creating an image for the new information. This can be done in various ways and is especially effective for visual learners. It can be as simple as drawing a picture that represents the word or new concept. Then, when you are attempting to retrieve the information, you can use the image to recall the information. The image should attach meaning to the word or concept. Many Science courses such as Biology require that students draw pictures of the terms and concepts on exams. Thus, this is an important part of the learning and study process to succeed on the test in those courses.

For other courses where the image might be more difficult to create—such as philosophy, you might consider creating a concept map that reveals the meaning of the word. In this visual, the term or concept would appear in relation to where it fits to other terms and concepts in the chapter. This will help you emphasize the interrelated and connectedness of the meaning of the term and concept. In the visual below, you will see two different types of visuals for quantitative data. The graph is a visual that shows what type of research quantitative research collects and depicts. The image of the two arrows shows that quantitative data are on the opposite spectrum of data collection as qualitative research.

**Figure 8.3: Back Side View of Concept Card Box 3**

| | |
|---|---|
| Quantitative methods use objective measurements and numerical analysis of data collected through polls, questionnaires or surveys (Babbie, 2010) | Quantitate methods believe that objective data can gathered and analyzed through processes such as surveys, polls, and questionnaires—emphasis is placed on numbers and measurements |
| 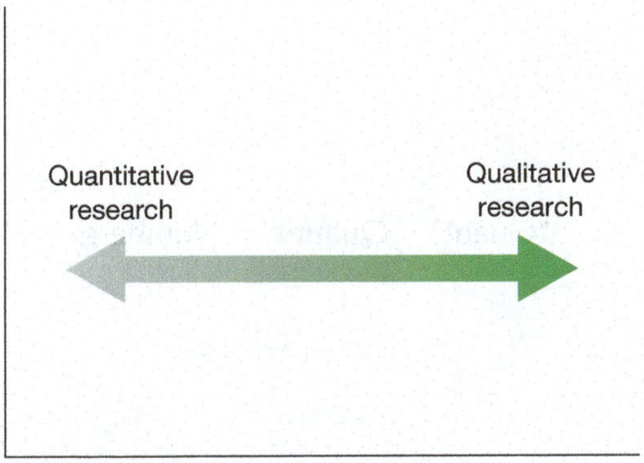  | |

For each of your new terms and concepts, create a visual representation in the third box of the concept card.

## Activity Four: Memory Devices

Attaching a memory trick, mnemonic device, or acronym to terms and concepts can also increase your chances for retrieving information from long-term memory. For example, SQ3R is a mnemonic device to help you remember the active reading strategy: survey, question (turn headings into questions), read (read each section to answer the heading questions in 1–2 sentences), respond (respond to the questions), and review (use the responses to write a chapter summary). A memory trick is any type of association you can form to help you remember the word. For example, Quant is embedded in Quantitative Research Methods. I would use this to remind me of "quantity" or counting, which would remind me that quantitative research methods place an emphasis on numbers.

Another strategy is to create an acronym or catch phrase. For example, musicians learned Every Good Boy Does Fine to remember the notes EGBDF. Or, FBI is another, which stands for the Federal Bureau of Investigation.

## Figure 8.4: Back Side View of Concept Card Box Four

<table>
<tr>
<td>Quantitative methods use objective measurements and numerical analysis of data collected through polls, questionnaires or surveys (Babbie, 2010)</td>
<td>Quantitate methods believe that objective data can gathered and analyzed through processes such as surveys, polls, and questionnaires—emphasis is placed on numbers and measurements</td>
</tr>
<tr>
<td>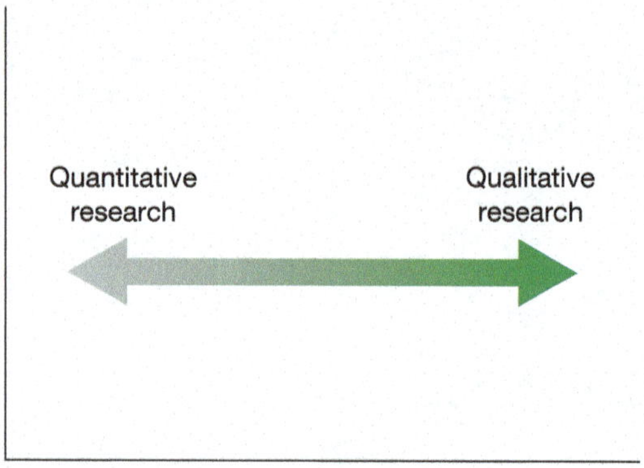
</td>
<td>"Quant" = Quantity = Numbers</td>
</tr>
</table>

In the last box of each of your concept cards, create a memory trick that will help you remember the new word or concept.

## References

Babbie, E. R. (2010). *The practice of social work* (12th Ed.). Belmont, CA: Wadsworth Cengage.

Bourne, L.E., Dominowski, E. F., & Healy, A. F. (1986). *Cognitive processes* (2nd Ed.). Englewood Cliffs, NJ: Prentice-Hall.

## Activity Five: Using Bloom's Taxonomy to Study

A common mistake that many college students make is only learning new material on the knowledge level of learning. The knowledge level is the lowest level of learning; on this level of learning, students learn information so that it can be recalled in its simplest form. For example, when you are asked to verify your phone number, address, and date of birth, you are recalling information on the knowledge level. In an exam, knowledge-level questions might appear as true/false or matching. However, only about 10% of test questions are knowledge-level questions. When students spend all of their time studying on this level, they are only preparing for about 10% of the exam questions. So, it is easy to see how students could spend 6 hours studying but still fail a test if they never study the information and anticipate questions at levels of learning beyond the knowledge level.

Bloom's Taxonomy has six levels of learning. Each level builds upon the prior level. The knowledge level is the lowest level of learning.

- **Knowledge-level questions:** Terms, facts, lists, dates
- **Comprehension:** Meaning
- **Application:** Apply to situation
- **Analysis:** Break down into parts/essay
- **Synthesis:** Combine ideas and information/essay
- **Evaluation:** Make judgments (often requires analysis and synthesis)

Studying in college requires that you learn material at all levels of Bloom's Taxonomy because college tests are written to test you on all these levels. Also, if you are in a major where you will take a licensure test at the end of your program, such as Nursing or Physical Therapy, you should know that Bloom's Taxonomy is used to write those tests as well. Beginning to study material on all levels of learning now will prepare you for studying for the licensure test later.

Learning concepts on all 6 levels ensures that you fully understand the concept. If you understand a concept on all levels of learning, you can succeed on any assessment. Use the following steps to check your understanding of the concept on all levels and prepare for class discussions, quizzes, and exams. It works best when you use your micro and macro time management skills (week one) and reading strategies (weeks six and seven) to identify key concepts and learn them on a regular basis. Then, studying for tests becomes review.

Use the following steps to practice learning with Bloom's Taxonomy.

1. Identify and note days/times on your study schedule where you can read the textbook with SQ3R, THIEVES, KWL. Make this a routine.
2. While reading the textbook identify and anticipate the most important concepts that you will need to know. These are the BIG concepts that are pivotal to understanding everything in the chapter/unit. Not all vocabulary terms are BIG concepts.
3. After class, review notes with your reading notes. In synthesizing notes with book notes, AGAIN identify the most important concepts. Which concepts are essential and most important to know? What was emphasized in class? Where was most of the lecture time spent? Examples offered?

4. For each of the most important concepts (BIG concepts), use the following chart to learn the concept on all levels of Bloom's Taxonomy. Write in each box.
5. Share aloud what you wrote in the chart with a classmate, friend, parent. Explaining the concept on each level aloud with someone else encodes meaning and ensures that you fully understand the concept.

**Figure 8.5: Bloom's Taxonomy of Learning**

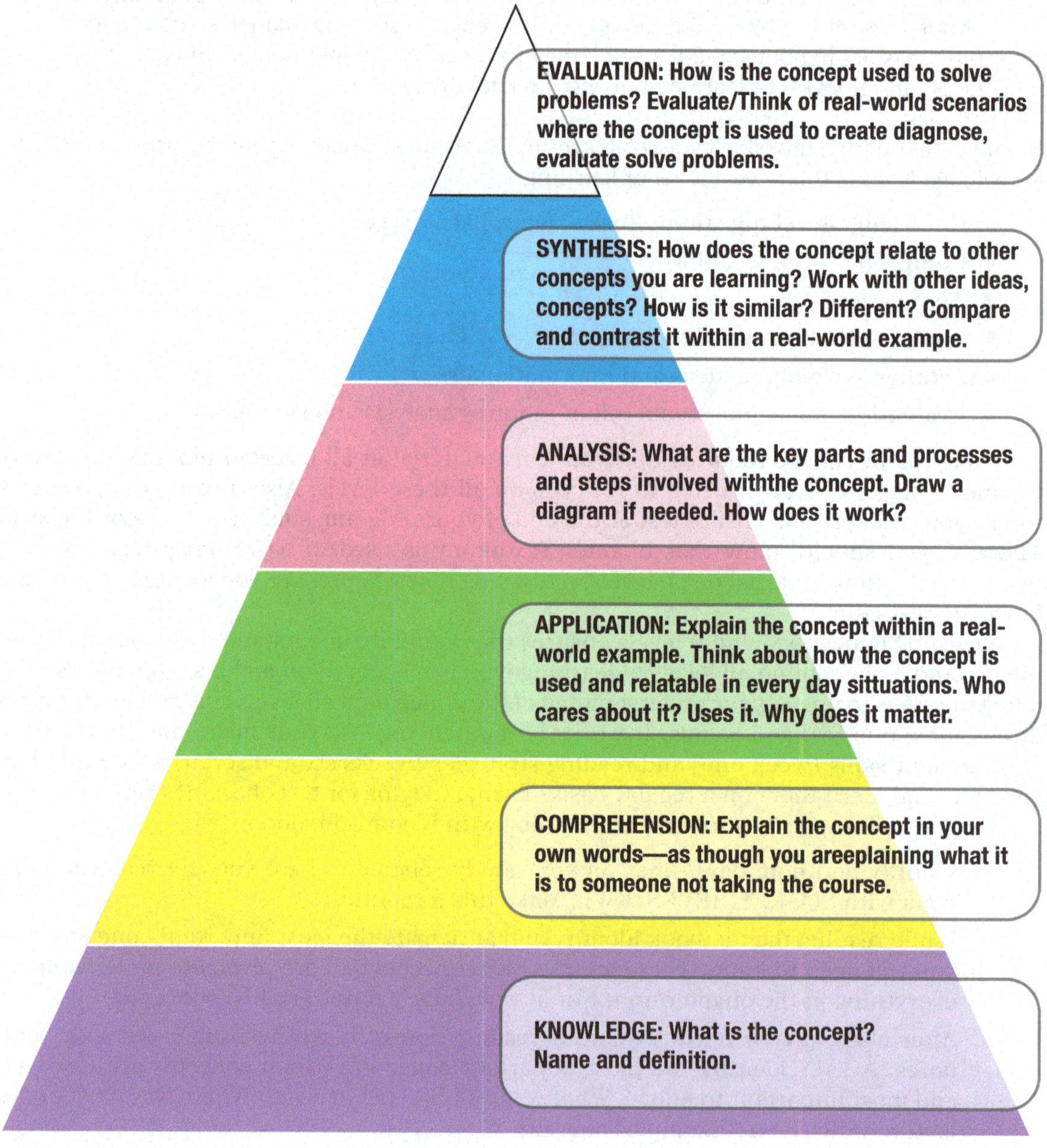

6. Use these steps routinely as new concepts are introduced during the time you established on your study schedule.

Successful students anticipate test questions and use self-testing methods to make sure they know course material on all levels of Bloom's Taxonomy. If you have been using the learning method described in Activity Five—the following activities should be more of a review for a test. Either way, writing test questions on all levels of learning in the types of questions that you have seen on prior tests in the course will allow you to practice demonstrating your understanding of the concepts on all 6 levels of learning. Most tests in college will assess you on all the levels of application and above. Few questions will be knowledge and comprehension level questions.

## Activity Six: Anticipating Knowledge-Level Questions

1. Purchase two packs of index cards. One should have five different colors. You can find these in any of the common retailers or office stores. Also, purchase a pack of white index cards. Together, the two packs of cards will give you six colors. You will designate one color for each level of Bloom's Taxonomy.

   Example:

   **White:** Knowledge

   **Blue:** Comprehension

   **Pink:** Application

   **Green:** Analysis

   **Yellow:** Synthesis

   **Purple:** Evaluation

2. Choose a chapter textbook from one of your courses. Review your textbook and class notes. As you look at the information, think back to previous tests. Of this information, which do you think will most likely appear as knowledge-level questions? Also, think about how many questions are on your tests. Ten percent of a 100-point test would be 10 points worth of questions. Based on this formula, how many knowledge-level questions might you expect?
3. Create some knowledge-level questions. Write the question on the front and the answer on the back.

**Knowledge Question:** What do professors use to write exams?

**Answer:** Bloom's Taxonomy

## Activity Seven: Creating Comprehension-Level Questions

Comprehension means that you not only know the information but also understand what it means. This means that you have encoded meaning in a way that has moved your learning beyond memorization.

1. In the same chapter that you anticipated knowledge-level questions, go back in and anticipate comprehension questions. Again, this is a lower level of learning. So, there will be less questions on this level of learning. Ten percent would be another good amount of questions to anticipate at this level.
2. On the color of card that you have designated for comprehension, write some comprehension-level questions. Again, write the question on the front and answer on the back.**Comprehension Question:** Why is only reviewing lecture notes not an effective study method in college?**Answer:** Reviewing lecture notes does not encode meaning, store information, or allow for recall. Thus, the information is not placed in long-term memory.

**Comprehension Question:** Why is only reviewing lecture notes not an effective study method in college?

**Answer:** Reviewing lecture notes does not encode meaning, store information, or allow for recall. Thus, the information is not placed in long-term memory.

## Activity Eight: Creating Application Questions

To apply information to other situations, knowledge and comprehension learning must have already occurred. Thus, applying meaning allows you to connect one information with another information. This makes learning more permanent. You can and should do this while you read. In fact, this is one way to make your reading and learning more interesting—apply your course material to your major or to the job that you would like to have in the future. Ask yourself, how is this related to what I want to do? How might I use this in the future? Or, how is this related to what I am learning in another class? The benefit of a liberal arts education is that interconnectedness of disciplines is emphasized and valued. Employers also seek this in employees. They prefer to hire individuals who can make connections!

1. In the same chapter that you have been anticipating questions, go back in and anticipate application questions. This is a higher level of learning. So, you should anticipate more of these questions. Again, think back to previous tests. How was this level of knowledge tested? Anticipate similar questions.
2. On the color of card that you have designated for application, write some application-level questions. Again, write the question on the front and answer on the back.**Application question:** In which of your classes, would it be best to read with SQ3R? Why?**Answer:** I use SQ3R for my Psychology course because the text has a lot of information organized by headings. The method allows me to efficiently pull out the main ideas.

**Application question:** In which of your classes, would it be best to read with SQ3R? Why?

**Answer:** I use SQ3R for my Psychology course because the text has a lot of information organized by headings. The method allows me to efficiently pull out the main ideas.

## Activity Nine: Creating Analysis-Level Questions

Analysis-level questions require you to break information into key parts to show understanding. They often ask that you identify main ideas and supporting details. For example, an analysis question in a History course might ask you to identify the main reasons the South attempted to secede from the North.

1. Using the same chapter, look for information that might be tested as analysis questions on your exam. Again, think back to previous tests. How was this level of knowledge tested? Anticipate similar questions.
2. On the color of card that you have designated for analysis, write some analysis-level questions. Again, write the question on the front and answer on the back.**Analysis Question:** How does information move from short-term memory to long-term memory? What study strategies are most effective in facilitating this process?**Answer:** For information to move from short-term memory to long-term memory, it must first be encoded, stored, and then retrieved. Study methods that attach meaning to new information and organize it in ways for easy retrieval are most effective. Concept cards facilitate this process; creating and quizzing yourself with Bloom's Taxonomy cards also facilitates moving information from short-term to long-term memory.

**Analysis Question:** How does information move from short-term memory to long-term memory? What study strategies are most effective in facilitating this process?

**Answer:** For information to move from short-term memory to long-term memory, it must first be encoded, stored, and then retrieved. Study methods that attach meaning to new information and organize it in ways for easy retrieval are most effective. Concept cards facilitate this process; creating and quizzing yourself with Bloom's Taxonomy cards also facilitates moving information from short-term to long-term memory.

## Activity Ten: Creating Synthesis Questions

Synthesis questions pull different ideas together to show how they are related and connected. For example, in a literature course, a synthesis question might ask you to find a common theme in two different stories. Or, in a literary analysis paper you might use Maslow's hierarchy of needs to analyze the actions of a character in a story. This would show a synthesis of Maslow's theories with your understanding of the character and the character's actions.

1. In the chapter you have been working on, which ideas and concepts might you be asked to compare and contrast to show synthesis? Often these types of questions ask that you compare (similarities) and contrast (differences).
2. On the color of card that you have designated for synthesis, write some synthesis-level questions. Again, write the question on the front and answer on the back.**Synthesis Question:** How does distorted thinking affect test-taking?**Answer:** Distorted thinking is not logical. It evokes an emotional response that creates anxiety. Anxiety causes the body to produce adrenaline and begin protecting itself, which shuts down cognitive activity. This can result in students not remembering or being able to retrieve information they have stored in their long-term memory.

**Synthesis Question:** How does distorted thinking affect test-taking?

**Answer:** Distorted thinking is not logical. It evokes an emotional response that creates anxiety. Anxiety causes the body to produce adrenaline and begin protecting itself, which shuts down cognitive activity. This can result in students not remembering or being able to retrieve information they have stored in their long-term memory.

## Activity Eleven: Creating Evaluation-Level Questions

Evaluation questions ask that you use the information you learned on the other levels to form judgments based on strengths and weaknesses.

1. As you look through the chapter, predict what types of evaluations you might be asked to make on the exam. How might you be asked to use the information and content to make judgments? This is a higher level of learning. So, you should anticipate more of these questions. Again, think back to previous tests. How was this level of knowledge tested? Anticipate similar questions.
2. On the color of card that you have designated for evaluation, write some evaluation-level questions. Again, write the question on the front and answer on the back.**Evaluation Question:** In which of the following situations, would THIEVES be the best reading strategy to use:

**Evaluation Question:** In which of the following situations, would THIEVES be the best reading strategy to use:

- **a.** Literature course requiring close reading
- **b.** Philosophy course with short essays assigned
- **c.** Lab reports for a Science course
- **d.** Biology textbook with headings, illustrations, and lots of vocabulary

**Answer:** D

## Activity Twelve: Bloom's Taxonomy Trivial Pursuit Group Study: Anticipating Test Questions

Students think that good studying involves long hours in the library with lots of memorization and recitation of facts. No wonder they dread it and avoid it! The reality is that learning is active, social, and can be fun! The following strategies actually involve a group—or at least a partner. Try them. Not only will they facilitate study that stores information in your long-term memory, you will feel like you are having too much fun to be studying!

Trivial Pursuit has six categories of questions. So does Bloom's Taxonomy! And, Bloom's Taxonomy forms the basis for the exams that your professors write. As you learned last week, it categorizes the understanding of material into six levels. The first level is the less complex, and the last is the most complex because it relies on all the prior levels.

## Bloom's Taxonomy

- **Knowledge-level questions:** Terms, facts, lists, dates
- **Comprehension:** Meaning
- **Application:** Apply to situation
- **Analysis:** Break down into parts/essay
- **Synthesis:** Combine ideas and information/essay
- **Evaluation:** Make judgments (often requires analysis and synthesis)

## Getting Started

1. Form a study group for one of your classes. Find a time and place to meet.
2. Have each group member bring two packs of index cards. One pack of five colors and one pack of white (see Week Eight). As a group, designate one color of card for each category of Bloom's Taxonomy. Example, blue might be the color for knowledge-level cards.
3. Ask each group member to write five questions for each level related to the current course chapter(s) being studied (five knowledge, five comprehension, five application, five analysis, five synthesis, and five evaluation). Write the questions on index cards. Each color should represent a different question type.
4. Collect all the questions and arrange them in piles by color. These will be your categories.
5. Roll a dice. The highest roll goes first. (You can form teams if you have a large number of students.) The student going first rolls the dice. The number indicates the question type. (1—knowledge, 2—comprehension, 3—application, 4—analysis, 5—synthesis, 6—evaluation).
6. Moving/scoring—If you have a trivial pursuit board, you could use it and play as you normally do. But, use your question cards as categories. Coordinate your categories to the pie pieces of trivial pursuit. If you do not have a board or wish to simplify, play to collect cards. The first to collect a card from each category wins. When questions are answered correctly, the player is allowed to continue rolling and answering from categories. Play ceases when a question is not answered correctly. You may also opt to play with the "phone a friend" option. *If this option is agreed upon at the beginning of the game, players are allowed to ask another player for advice. However, if they choose this option and answer incorrectly, they must return one of their cards to the pile.*

## Activity Thirteen: Apples to Apples—Learning Vocabulary and Key Concepts

This strategy applies your course concepts and vocabulary to the content of the popular game—Apples to Apples. It also creates multiple connections and problem solving, which facilitates long-term memory and learning of the material.

1. Form a study group for one of your classes. Agree on a time and place to meet. Have group members bring textbooks, notes, and two different colors of index cards. You should agree on the two colors of cards.
2. Create concept cards for the key terms and concepts in your chapter (See Week Seven). Use two different colors of index cards.
   - ❖ Use one color for key headings of your textbook chapter or notes. These would be the major concepts. Write a brief sentence describing the concept that will jog your memory. You may also want to include a picture. Divide up the headings/concepts, assigning some to each group member.
   - ❖ Use the other color for vocabulary or concepts that fall below the headings. On the back of the cards, draw a large cross that creates four boxes. Use the boxes to define the word in four different ways: (1) textbook definition, (2) define in your own words, (3) picture or visual representation, and (4) memory trick/mnemonic device. Again, divide this task up by group members. Group members may already have concept cards/vocabulary cards created on index cards. If so, create one large, shuffled pile of the cards.
3. Place the cards in two different piles. Organize by color. Place headings in one pile and vocabulary/concepts in another.
4. Each player should choose five vocabulary cards.
5. Take turns being the judge. Like Apples to Apples, the judge places one of the heading cards in the center of the table and announces the heading. Players choose one vocabulary card that they feel best relates—hoping the judge will choose their card.
6. The judge places each card he or she was given on the table for all to see and verbally discusses how the card relates or does not relate—eventually deciding on the best fit and his or her reasoning.
7. The player who had the best fit receives the heading card. The first player to receive five heading cards wins.

## Activity Fourteen: Studying Taboo Style

This game is based on the same premise of Taboo. You have a word that you need to get another person to say—but many of the words you usually use to describe it are on list of words you cannot say. This forces you to create new connections and new ways of thinking about course words and concepts—which fosters long-term memory and learning.

1. Form a study group of at least four members. Agree on a time and place to meet.
2. **Create cards.** Use index cards to create concept cards of vocabulary and key concepts. (If your group members already have cards created, use those cards. Adapt them by restricting any words from the definitions on the back.)
   - ❖ On the front of the card, list the vocabulary word or concept.
   - ❖ On the back of the card, list common words associated with the word. Include words from the definition. (These are the words that will not be allowed to be spoken as clues).
3. **Form teams.** Divide into teams. (This is why you need at least four study partners.) Combine the cards into one pile.
4. **Roles.** One team begins by deciding who will be the clue giver and who will be the guesser. The clue giver takes the pile of cards and begins with the card on top of the pile. The clue giver quickly reads the word and then looks at the back of the card.
5. **Play begins.** The clue giver must give clues and talk about the word in a way that will allow the guesser to identify the word/concept. But—the clue giver **cannot** use any of the words listed on the back of the card. A member from the other team stands behind the clue giver to make sure the words on the back are not used and to keep track of time. Each time one of the words is used, the judge from the other team marks a tally and announces that the word cannot be used. The tallies become points that are deducted from the total score earned in the round. The clue giver is only allowed 3 minutes for giving clues and to get through as many cards as possible in that time frame. Cards can be skipped, but one point is deducted for each skipped card.
6. **Earning points.** Points are earned for each card that is guessed correctly; one point per card. When a card is guessed correctly, it is placed in a pile, and the clue giver should quickly move on to the next card, in an attempt to get through as many cards as possible in the 3 minutes allowed.
7. **Winning.** Teams continue to take turns guessing words and switching roles until the agreed upon points are reached by a team.

**Weekly Goals** **Week of:** ______________________________

**What am I grateful for?**

**What are your goal(s) for the week?**

| Course: | ________ | ________ | ________ | ________ | ________ | ________ |
|---|---|---|---|---|---|---|
| • To do: | | | | | | |
| • Strateg(ies): | | | | | | |
| • Resource(s): | | | | | | |

**Personal Wellness/Spirituality:**

**Family & Friends:**

## Weekly Planner

**Week of:** ______________________

| | Monday | Tuesday | Wednesday | Thursday | Friday | Saturday | Sunday |
|---|---|---|---|---|---|---|---|
| 06:00 am | | | | | | | |
| 06:30 am | | | | | | | |
| 07:00 am | | | | | | | |
| 07:30 am | | | | | | | |
| 08:00 am | | | | | | | |
| 08:30 am | | | | | | | |
| 09:00 am | | | | | | | |
| 09:30 am | | | | | | | |
| 10:00 am | | | | | | | |
| 10:30 am | | | | | | | |
| 11:00 am | | | | | | | |
| 11:30 am | | | | | | | |
| 12:00 pm | | | | | | | |
| 12:30 pm | | | | | | | |
| 01:00 pm | | | | | | | |
| 01:30 pm | | | | | | | |
| 02:00 pm | | | | | | | |
| 02:30 pm | | | | | | | |
| 03:00 pm | | | | | | | |
| 03:30 pm | | | | | | | |
| 04:00 pm | | | | | | | |
| 04:30 pm | | | | | | | |
| 05:00 pm | | | | | | | |
| 05:30 pm | | | | | | | |
| 06:00 pm | | | | | | | |
| 06:30 pm | | | | | | | |
| 07:00 pm | | | | | | | |
| 07:30 pm | | | | | | | |
| 08:00 pm | | | | | | | |
| 08:30 pm | | | | | | | |
| 09:00 pm | | | | | | | |
| 09:30 pm | | | | | | | |
| 10:00 pm | | | | | | | |
| 10:30 pm | | | | | | | |

## Important Thoughts / Things to Remember / Doodling

Week Nine

# Metacognition— Rethinking and Revisioning the Learning and Study Plan

Successful students engage in metacognition. Metacognition involves thinking about your current processes, habits, and activities and making adjustments to find greater success.

Midterm is the perfect time to re-think and revise your learning and study plan to find great success.

The metacognitive activities in Week 9 will aid you revising your learning and study plans.

## Activity One: Self-Assess

1. Use the self-assessment from Week One to reflect on your growth—now that you have been implementing new strategies.

## Figure 9.1: Self-Assessment

**Date:**

(5 is highest)

**1.** How are you feeling about your skills in the following areas:

| | | | | | |
|---|---|---|---|---|---|
| Reading | 1 | 2 | 3 | 4 | 5 |
| Writing | 1 | 2 | 3 | 4 | 5 |
| Note-Taking | 1 | 2 | 3 | 4 | 5 |
| Time Management | 1 | 2 | 3 | 4 | 5 |
| Organization | 1 | 2 | 3 | 4 | 5 |
| Test-Taking | 1 | 2 | 3 | 4 | 5 |
| Oral Communication | 1 | 2 | 3 | 4 | 5 |
| Studying | 1 | 2 | 3 | 4 | 5 |
| Motivation | 1 | 2 | 3 | 4 | 5 |

For those that are not "5," what do you feel would help you get to a "5"?

Which skill areas have most impacted your success in the past?
How can this course help?

**2.** How do you feel about taking this course? Why?

3. What strategies will you use in this course to be successful?

4. What technology needs do you have? How might you address these needs? What gaps may still exist?

5. What challenges do you have this semester that might impact your success in this course that your professor should be aware of? How do you plan to meet these challenges? (Make a plan for communicating needs with professor).

6. What resources will you use to be successful in this course (Ex. Writing Center, Learning Center, Counseling Center, Library, Campus Ministry, IT, Compass/Career Center)?

7. What goals do you wish to make for this semester? What support do you need to achieve these goals?

2. After completing the self-assessment, respond to the following questions:
   - ❖ Where have you seen the greatest growth?
   - ❖ What new strategies have contributed to this growth? How will you keep this growth going by continuing to practice the strategies?
   - ❖ Where do you still need to grow?
   - ❖ What adjustments/changes could you make to improve in the areas that still need growth?
   - ❖ What strategies, resources or support would help you to improve?
   - ❖ What is your plan for implementing these new strategies and resources?
3. Review your study schedule.
   - ❖ What adjustments do you need to make to your study schedule to make the changes you committed to in question 2?
   - ❖ Make new adjustments to your study schedule.
4. Review your learning plan.
   - ❖ What adjustments do you need to make to your learning plan? What new strategies should be integrated? New resources?

## Activity Two: Staying on Track: Using a Grade Calculator

While learning should be the focus of your education, grades often determine if you will be allowed into majors and programs. They also determine if students are eligible for athletics, make the Dean's List, and ultimately, if students get to stay at a university to continue their learning.

A grade calculator can help you plan for the grade goals needed for you to succeed and meet the requirements necessary for your plans.

Use the following grade calculator and (or another you prefer) to track your progress in your classes.

- ♦ https://gpacalculator.io/cumulative-gpa-calculator/
- ♦ Begin by entering realistic grade goals for each of your courses. Your midterm grades should give you a good estimate of what you might finish with for a final grade in the course. Use the following questions to guide you in setting realistic grade goals:
   - ❖ If you make the adjustments from Activity One (new strategies and resources) how might your grade change?
   - ❖ What assignments are still out for the last half of the semester that will be factored into the final grade? What percentage of the final grade are these assignments?
   - ❖ Based on your strengths and weaknesses and new use of strategies and resources, how might you do on these assignments?
   - ❖ How might you begin working/meeting more closely with the professor?
   - ❖ What extra credit opportunities could you take advantage of to improve the grade?
   - ❖ Are there opportunities to revise assignments that you might take advantage of to improve your grade?

- ❖ Are you able to pass the class? Do you need to withdraw? What are the deadlines for withdrawing?
- ❖ **STEP 1:** How might meeting with your advisor be helpful?

♦ Note your semester GPA goal.

♦ Note your cumulative GPA goal.

♦ What additional revisions might you make to your learning and study plans based on these goals? (Week 9: Activity One).

## Activity Three: Post-Test Analysis

Conducting a post-test analysis after you take a test is another important metacognitive practice. Analyzing what went wrong with the questions you missed on a test, can help you improve your test-taking, learning, and studying practices—and thus help you to improve your performance on future tests.

Use the following steps to analyze your test performance. If you don't get to keep your tests in a course, make an appointment with your professor to work through the following steps in a meeting with your professor and better understand your test performance.

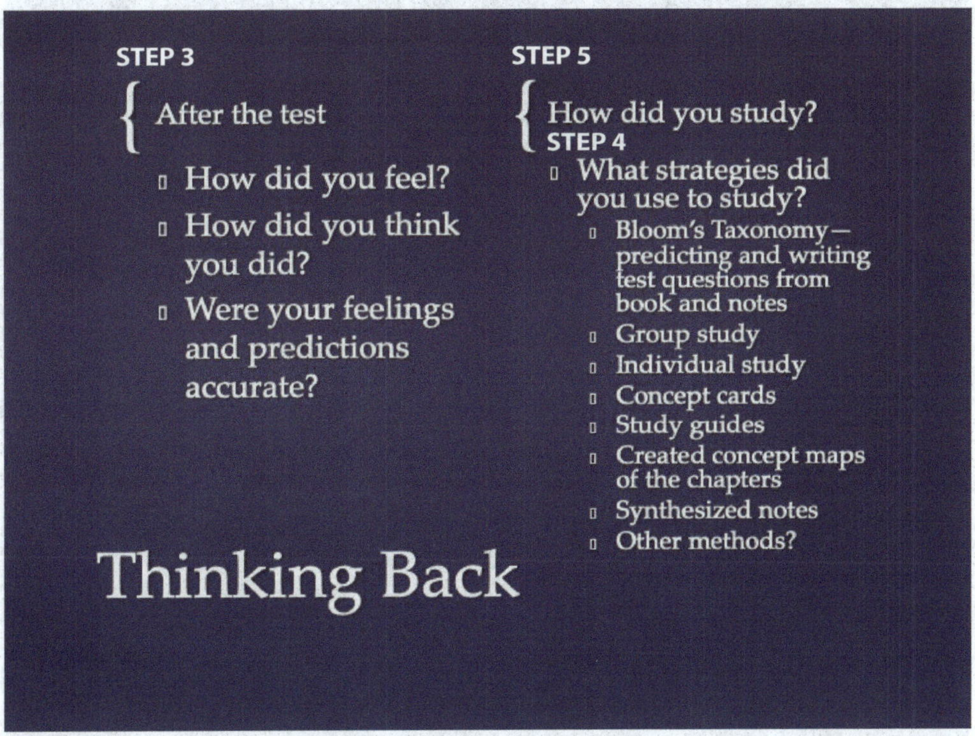

STEP 2

**Look at the test questions**

- For each question identify where it came from:
  - Book (B)
  - In-class notes (C)
  - Online materials (O)
  - Not sure (?)

**Adding it all up**

- Count the number of questions in each category
- Which question types did you miss most often?
- Compare this with your study methods
- What adjustments might you make based on this information?

## An Analysis of the Test—Where the Information Came From

**Question type: Identify each question type on the test**

- Knowledge-level questions
- Comprehension
- Application
- Analysis
- Synthesis
- Evaluation

**Adding it all up**

- Count the number of questions in each category
- Which question types did you miss most often?
- Compare this with your study methods
- What adjustments might you make based on this information?

## An Analysis of the test—What type of questions did you miss most often?

STEP 6

## Bloom's Taxonomy

- Knowledge-level questions
- Comprehension
- Application
- Analysis
- Synthesis
- Evaluation

## 6 Levels of Knowing

- Terms, facts, lists, dates
- Meaning
- Apply to situation
- Break down into parts/essay
- Combine ideas and information/essay
- Make judgments (often requires analysis and synthesis)

# Studying for Understanding

STEP 7

## New Plan

- Based on the analysis of your test performance, make a new plan for studying for the next test.
- What will you do differently?

## Need help sorting it out?

- Make an appointment with the Learning Center or your professor

# Making a Plan

## Activity Four: Adjusting Goals

Successful students set and monitor goals. Engaging in metacognitive practices means that you also adjust goals as you reflect on what is working and not working. This week, you have been engaging in metacognition as you assessed yourself, monitored your grade progress, analyzed your tests and made changes to your learning and study plans.

How will the new changes and adjustments you have added to your learning and study plans impact your goals? Review your goals that you set on the Goal setting chart from week one.

Use the chart below to make new goals or make adjustments to your goals.

## Figure 9.2: Goal Setting

Most Students find success when they make adjustments in the following areas. Use the chart to evaluate yourself in these areas and set some goals. **Example of a specific goal that could be demonstrated and assessed: Time Management: I will create a "to do" list each Sunday and write what I need to get done on my planner for the week.**

**Goal that is too general: Use my time effectively.**

| | | |
|---|---|---|
| **Reading**<br><br>**SMI INFP** | **Strengths:**<br><br>**Weaknesses:** | **Goals** |
| **Organization**<br><br>**MOT ANX TMT ATT** | **Strengths:**<br><br>**Weaknesses:** | **Goals** |
| **Studying**<br><br>**SFT UAR** | **Strengths:**<br><br>**Weaknesses:** | **Goals** |
| **Test-Taking**<br><br>**TST UAR** | **Strengths:**<br><br>**Weaknesses:** | **Goals** |
| **Time Management**<br><br>**TST UAR** | **Strengths:**<br><br>**Weaknesses:** | **Goals** |
| **Oral Communication**<br><br>**INFP SMI ANX ATT UAR** | **Strengths:**<br><br>**Weaknesses:** | **Goals** |
| **Motivation/Growth Mindset**<br><br>**MOT ANX ATT** | **Strengths:**<br><br>**Weaknesses:** | **Goals** |

**Weekly Goals** **Week of:** ____________________

**What am I grateful for?**

**What are your goal(s) for the week?**

| **Course:** | ______ | ______ | ______ | ______ | ______ | ______ |
|---|---|---|---|---|---|---|
| • To do: | | | | | | |
| • Strateg(ies): | | | | | | |
| • Resource(s): | | | | | | |

**Personal Wellness/Spirituality:**

**Family & Friends:**

**Weekly Planner** **Week of:** ______________________

| | Monday | Tuesday | Wednesday | Thursday | Friday | Saturday | Sunday |
|---|---|---|---|---|---|---|---|
| 06:00 am | | | | | | | |
| 06:30 am | | | | | | | |
| 07:00 am | | | | | | | |
| 07:30 am | | | | | | | |
| 08:00 am | | | | | | | |
| 08:30 am | | | | | | | |
| 09:00 am | | | | | | | |
| 09:30 am | | | | | | | |
| 10:00 am | | | | | | | |
| 10:30 am | | | | | | | |
| 11:00 am | | | | | | | |
| 11:30 am | | | | | | | |
| 12:00 pm | | | | | | | |
| 12:30 pm | | | | | | | |
| 01:00 pm | | | | | | | |
| 01:30 pm | | | | | | | |
| 02:00 pm | | | | | | | |
| 02:30 pm | | | | | | | |
| 03:00 pm | | | | | | | |
| 03:30 pm | | | | | | | |
| 04:00 pm | | | | | | | |
| 04:30 pm | | | | | | | |
| 05:00 pm | | | | | | | |
| 05:30 pm | | | | | | | |
| 06:00 pm | | | | | | | |
| 06:30 pm | | | | | | | |
| 07:00 pm | | | | | | | |
| 07:30 pm | | | | | | | |
| 08:00 pm | | | | | | | |
| 08:30 pm | | | | | | | |
| 09:00 pm | | | | | | | |
| 09:30 pm | | | | | | | |
| 10:00 pm | | | | | | | |
| 10:30 pm | | | | | | | |

# Important Thoughts / Things to Remember / Doodling

## Week Ten

# Note-Taking Strategies that Make a Difference

Students know they should take notes, but they aren't sure what is important to write down—so they try to write down everything. Often, this creates pages and pages of unorganized chaos when they go back and try to study from their notes.

Another problem is that many professors use PowerPoint slides and make them accessible to students. Thus, some students believe the slides cover it all, so they don't take notes.

If you remember the information processing model, you don't place new information into your short memory and move it into long-term memory unless you encode it with meaning, store it, and retrieve it.

Taking effective notes is the first step to encoding new information by attaching meaning to it. And taking notes in an organized manner that embeds methods of retrieval and recall into the system allows you to move the information from short-term memory into your long-term memory. Two effective strategies that are known to facilitate this process and lead students to academic success in college are Quiz Notes and Cornell Notes.

## Quiz Notes

- Fold a sheet of notebook paper so that the left side of the paper, when folded, divides the paper in half.

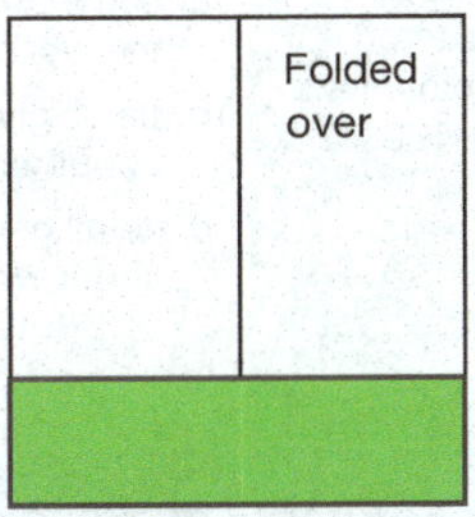


- At the bottom of the sheet of the paper, draw a horizontal line that will allow for you enough space to write at least two paragraphs.

- ♦ Listen for key words and transition words to create an informal outline of the lecture.
- ♦ In the right hand column of the paper, place key topics as Roman numerals.
  - ❖ For example, if the professor says "We are going to begin with unemployment trends in the US during the 1900s." You would write:

    **I.** Unemployment Trends/US 1900s
- ♦ Place supporting details as numbered points under the Roman numeral.
  - ❖ For example, the instructor might say "More women began to enter the workforce." You would write:

    **I.** Unemployment Trends/US 1900s

    **1.** Women

    **a.** began to enter the workforce

    **b.** detail given about women

    **c.** detail given about women
- ♦ Create new roman numerals or subpoints under unemployment trends as the professor introduces new topics. Listen for shifts in topic. For example, the instructor might indicate a new topic by saying "another unemployment trend was immigration" or "Moving on to the Industrialization of the Workforce." You would write: 2. Immigrants; II. Industrialization of the Workforce.
- ♦ After class, review the notes. In the left hand margin, write a test question that your notes would answer for each section of the outline. For example, Opposite I. you might write "What were three ways that women impacted unemployment?"
- ♦ At the bottom of the sheet of the paper, write a brief summary of the class notes in your own words in about two paragraphs. In your summary, condense the notes to the main concepts and themes.

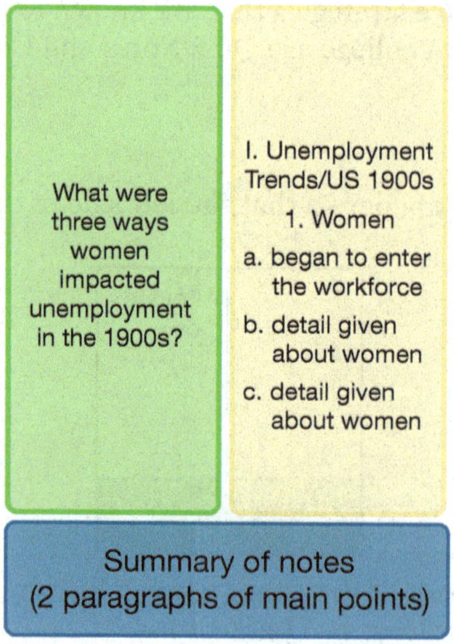

- When studying, fold the right hand side of the paper in half to cover the answers to the questions. Use the left hand side questions to quiz yourself, and check yourself with the notes in the outline.

## PowerPoint Slides

- When PowerPoints are used, after class convert the notes to the quiz notes format. This will allow you to put the notes into your own words, which will transfer the information to short-term and long-term memory.

## Bloom's Taxonomy

To add Bloom's Taxonomy to your Quiz Notes, you could challenge yourself to write questions in the left hand margin on all levels of Bloom's Taxonomy. Anticipate how the lecture material might appear on the test in the six levels and create questions of that format. Highlight the questions with six different colors. One color could represent each level of the taxonomy.

## Activity One: Taking Notes with Quiz Notes

1. Choose a page of notes or a set of PowerPoint slides from one of your courses.
2. Convert your notes to Quiz Notes.
3. Use the method for taking notes in the next course lecture for that class.

Reflection:

What did you like about this note taking method?

________________________________________

________________________________________

________________________________________

How might using it in the future increase your learning?

________________________________________

________________________________________

Which classes would this method work best for? Why?

________________________________________

________________________________________

### Cornell Notes

Cornell Notes is similar to Quiz Notes in that it outlines the important information of the lecture on the right hand side of the page. However, with Cornell Notes, you don't fold the page. Instead, you draw a vertical line down the center of the page. And, on the left hand side of the page, you don't write questions. Instead, you summarize the information on the right hand side into key ideas and phrases. So opposite the information on the right, you write on the left key words or short phrases that summarize the information. At the bottom of the page, you also draw a horizontal line. And, after class in that space, you summarize the notes in your own words in about two paragraphs. The key words and short phrases on the left hand side help you to identify what is most important to include in the summary.

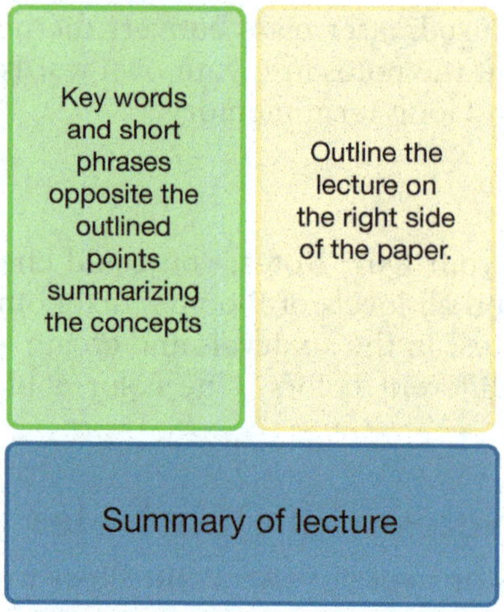


## Activity Two: Taking Notes with Cornell Notes

1. Choose a page of notes or a set of PowerPoint slides from one of your courses.
2. Convert your notes to Cornell Notes.
3. Use the method for taking notes in the next course lecture for that class.

Reflection:

What did you like about this note-taking method?

________________________________________

________________________________________

________________________________________

How might using it in the future increase your learning?

________________________________________

________________________________________

Which classes would this method work best for? Why?

________________________________________

________________________________________

## Activity Three: Note Reduction

One of the most effective study techniques before an exam is note reduction. Note reduction forces you to reduce all your notes (about 1 week before an exam) to first a sheet of paper, then to a half sheet of paper, and finally to an index card. In order to do this, you need to process the information on a high level and make some serious decisions about the information. What ends up on the index card should aid you in recalling anything that is essential to know for the test? How do you do this? You begin by going back to the learning objectives for the unit. What has your professor established as learning objectives? These tell you what is most important for you to know and should guide you in the note reduction process.

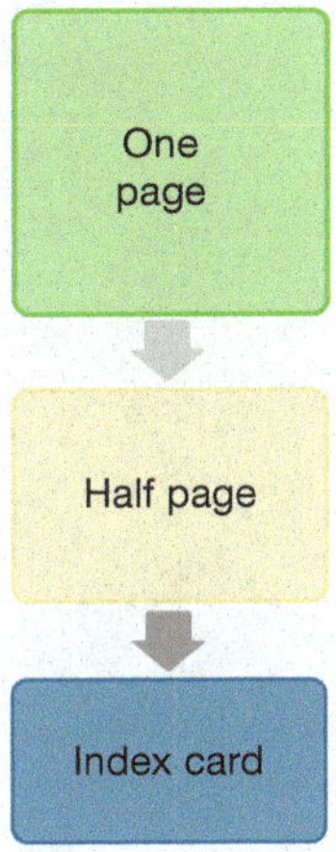


Step One: Choose a course you have a test coming up in soon—about a week or so.

Step Two: Reduce all your notes for the test to one page. (You may find using concept maps or SmartArt in Word or PowerPoint a useful tool for reducing and synthesizing notes. Reorganizing information into charts, graphs, and visuals can be a powerful for studying, reducing, and remembering.)

Step Three: Reduce the notes from your one page of reduction to half a page of notes.

Step Four: Reduce the half page of notes to an index card of notes.

Reflection:

What was most challenging about note reduction?

______________________________________________

______________________________________________

______________________________________________

How did it increase your learning of the material?

______________________________________________________________________

______________________________________________________________________

______________________________________________________________________

How will you use it in the future?

______________________________________________________________________

______________________________________________________________________

______________________________________________________________________

Talent wins games, but teamwork and intelligence win championships.

**— Michael Jordan**

**Weekly Goals** **Week of:** ____________________

**What am I grateful for?**

**What are your goal(s) for the week?**

| **Course:** | ________ | ________ | ________ | ________ | ________ | ________ |
|---|---|---|---|---|---|---|
| • To do: | | | | | | |
| • Strateg(ies): | | | | | | |
| • Resource(s): | | | | | | |

**Personal Wellness/Spirituality:**

**Family & Friends:**

**Weekly Planner** **Week of:** ____________________

| | Monday | Tuesday | Wednesday | Thursday | Friday | Saturday | Sunday |
|---|---|---|---|---|---|---|---|
| 06:00 am | | | | | | | |
| 06:30 am | | | | | | | |
| 07:00 am | | | | | | | |
| 07:30 am | | | | | | | |
| 08:00 am | | | | | | | |
| 08:30 am | | | | | | | |
| 09:00 am | | | | | | | |
| 09:30 am | | | | | | | |
| 10:00 am | | | | | | | |
| 10:30 am | | | | | | | |
| 11:00 am | | | | | | | |
| 11:30 am | | | | | | | |
| 12:00 pm | | | | | | | |
| 12:30 pm | | | | | | | |
| 01:00 pm | | | | | | | |
| 01:30 pm | | | | | | | |
| 02:00 pm | | | | | | | |
| 02:30 pm | | | | | | | |
| 03:00 pm | | | | | | | |
| 03:30 pm | | | | | | | |
| 04:00 pm | | | | | | | |
| 04:30 pm | | | | | | | |
| 05:00 pm | | | | | | | |
| 05:30 pm | | | | | | | |
| 06:00 pm | | | | | | | |
| 06:30 pm | | | | | | | |
| 07:00 pm | | | | | | | |
| 07:30 pm | | | | | | | |
| 08:00 pm | | | | | | | |
| 08:30 pm | | | | | | | |
| 09:00 pm | | | | | | | |
| 09:30 pm | | | | | | | |
| 10:00 pm | | | | | | | |
| 10:30 pm | | | | | | | |

## Important Thoughts / Things to Remember / Doodling

Week Eleven

# Life Management: Applying Covey's First Three Habits to College

Stephen Covey (2004) is well known for his book *The 7 Habits of Highly Effective People*. From his book, an institute, planners, and a store have emerged. Many companies even send their employees to the Covey Institute to be trained in the Covey system because it is more than a time management system. It is a life management system that is holistic and encourages you to bring balance and order to your life. And, when people commit to the habits, they find powerful and successful change in their lives. This week, we will apply Covey's first three habits to academic life in college.

## Habit 1: Be Proactive!

Covey (2004) explains in his book that proactive people respond rather than react. Responders are able to take a step back in the midst of challenges, take a deep breath, and look at the big picture. They are able to think about the most productive and effective course of action—and then take it. Reactors are governed by their emotions. In the face of challenges, they let their emotions determine their actions and words. They don't think things through—as a result, they are often left to deal with consequences they didn't anticipate nor want.

For example, a college student fails an Algebra test.

Response: Wow. That wasn't what I anticipated. I need to figure out what went wrong. I will set up an appointment with my professor to go over the test and find a better method for studying for the next test. I will also set up an appointment with one of the Math coaches in the Learning Center to go over my homework.

Reaction: That sucks! I am such an idiot. I have never been good at Math. And, my professor never teaches. I give up.

Would the response or reaction find greater success in the future? Not surprisingly, responders tend to succeed in college.

## Activity One: Responding Rather Than Reacting

1. List all the courses you are taking below:

   ____________________________

   ____________________________

   ____________________________

   ____________________________

   ____________________________

2. Beside each course, write whether you tend to react or respond in that course.
3. For the courses that you are reacting in, problem solve why you are reacting rather than responding. Then, list one thing you will do in the course this week to be more of a responder.

   ❖ **Course reacting in:**

   **Reasons:**

   **One step of response for this week:**

   ❖ **Course reacting in:**

   **Reasons:**

   **One step of response for this week:**

   ❖ **Course reacting in:**

   **Reasons:**

   **One step of response for this week:**

## Habit 2: Begin with the End in Mind

Covey (2004) challenged us in habit 2 to begin with the end in mind. In order to do this, you need to know who you want to be. This is much bigger than figuring out your major—but it is directly linked. In imagining who you want to be, Covey (2004) said to think of what people say about you after you die at your funeral. What do you want people to remember you for? What do you want to have accomplished? What kinds of things would you want to hear them say about you? Use this to help you understand what you really stand for and value. Then, write your own personal mission. Much like a business (or your college) uses a mission statement to stay focused, you will use your mission to create focus in your life. So, take your mission seriously.

## Activity Two: Writing Your Mission Statement

1. What do you want others to say about you after you have passed away? What kind of person do you want to be described as? What do you want to have accomplished?

   List these things below:

   ______________________________________________

   ______________________________________________

   ______________________________________________

   ______________________________________________

   ______________________________________________

   ______________________________________________

2. Now read through your list. What values and themes do you see? Use this to write a mission statement for yourself.

   ______________________________________________

   ______________________________________________

   ______________________________________________

   The mission statement is intended to keep you focused and should always be kept in a place that is prominent as you plan each week and day. It will help you remember what is most important as you balance the various roles that you play in your life.

3. List the roles that you play in your life. For example, are you a student? employee? athlete? daughter? son? mother? father? brother? sister? friend? spouse? girlfriend? boyfriend? List as many roles as apply. Then, beside each role set a goal you will work on in that role to help you achieve your overall mission.

| Roles | Goals |
|---|---|
| ____________________ | ____________________ |
| ____________________ | ____________________ |
| ____________________ | ____________________ |
| ____________________ | ____________________ |
| ____________________ | ____________________ |
| ____________________ | ____________________ |

**Habit #2: Begin With the End in Mind**

- Imagine—Who do you want to be?
- Become who you want to be.

Reflect 1: What is your personal mission?

Reflect 2: What roles do you play? And what goals can you set for each role to achieve your mission?

Example: Role → Student
Mission: To be known for my work.
Goal: Produce quality work in my classes.

## Habit 3: Put First Things First

Covey's (2004) third habit teaches us that productive people are not products of their time. Rather, productive people learn how to manage themselves and make effective choices about how they will spend their time. Having a mission to govern your life and keeping it always in mind with respect to the roles that you play helps you to make choices about how you invest your time to achieve your mission.

The famous metaphor that Covey (2004) used to further explain this is the rocks and the jar. If you have several large rocks and sand to fit into a jar, you will never fit all of it in the jar by shoving it all in together without a plan. In fact, you will likely not fit most of the large rocks into the jar.

Think of the large rocks as what is most important in your life—the roles you play. The sand is all of the extra little stuff. The rocks are most important to you, so they must go in the jar first! Then, all of the sand (the little extra things that are less important) can slide in around them.

## Activity Three: The Rocks

For each of your roles, what is most important for you to do today? This week? List each role. Then, for each role also list the tasks that you must do today and this week.

In your role as student, what is most important for you to do this week?

| Role | Task: Today | Task: this Week |
| --- | --- | --- |
| Student | Turn in Research Paper | Study for Chemistry |
| | | |
| | | |
| | | |
| | | |

| Role | Task: Today | Task: this Week |
| --- | --- | --- |
| | | |
| | | |
| | | |
| | | |
| | | |

## Activity Four: Emotional Bank Account

With the emotional bank account, Covey (2004) challenged us to make more deposits than withdrawals in our relationships.

Students make withdrawals when they fail to attend class, don't prepare for class, speak to classmates in class while the professor is talking, don't turn in assignments, disrupt other students' learning in class, repeatedly arrive late to class, or respond to professors and other students in unprofessional and disrespectful ways. Students make deposits by coming to class prepared, turning in assignments on time, utilizing office hours, building rapport and relationships with students, attending class, participating in class, and treating their classmates and their professor with respect and professionalism.

Successful students strive to maintain positive emotional bank accounts in all of their roles.

**Trust: Emotional Bank Account**

| Deposit | Withdrawals |
|---|---|
| • Kindness and respect<br>• Follow through on promises<br>• Clear expectations and communication<br>• Loyalty<br>• Sincere apology/humility | • Disrespect and unkindness<br>• Don't uphold promises/ no follow through<br>• Unclear<br>• Insincerity, dishonesty, lack of loyalty<br>• Arrogance |

1. List each of your roles. Use the chart below to assess where your emotional bank account balance is for each of your roles. Place a + beside it if you have a positive balance (make more deposits than withdrawals); place a negative beside it if you have a negative balance (make more withdrawals than deposits).

| Role | Balance [+ /–] |
|---|---|
| | |
| | |
| | |
| | |
| | |
| | |

2. For the roles that you have a negative balance, list one deposit you can make this week to begin rebuilding the account.

| Role | Deposit |
|---|---|
| | |
| | |
| | |
| | |
| | |
| | |

## Reference


Covey, S. R. (2004). *The 7 habits of highly effective people: Powerful lessons in personal change*. New York: Free Press.

Education is the most powerful weapon which you can use to change the world.

**— Nelson Mandela**

## Weekly Goals

**Week of:** ____________________

**What am I grateful for?**

**What are your goal(s) for the week?**

| **Course:** | ______ | ______ | ______ | ______ | ______ | ______ |
|---|---|---|---|---|---|---|
| • To do: | | | | | | |
| • Strateg(ies): | | | | | | |
| • Resource(s): | | | | | | |

**Personal Wellness/Spirituality:**

**Family & Friends:**

**Weekly Planner** **Week of:** ______________________

| | Monday | Tuesday | Wednesday | Thursday | Friday | Saturday | Sunday |
|---|---|---|---|---|---|---|---|
| 06:00 am | | | | | | | |
| 06:30 am | | | | | | | |
| 07:00 am | | | | | | | |
| 07:30 am | | | | | | | |
| 08:00 am | | | | | | | |
| 08:30 am | | | | | | | |
| 09:00 am | | | | | | | |
| 09:30 am | | | | | | | |
| 10:00 am | | | | | | | |
| 10:30 am | | | | | | | |
| 11:00 am | | | | | | | |
| 11:30 am | | | | | | | |
| 12:00 pm | | | | | | | |
| 12:30 pm | | | | | | | |
| 01:00 pm | | | | | | | |
| 01:30 pm | | | | | | | |
| 02:00 pm | | | | | | | |
| 02:30 pm | | | | | | | |
| 03:00 pm | | | | | | | |
| 03:30 pm | | | | | | | |
| 04:00 pm | | | | | | | |
| 04:30 pm | | | | | | | |
| 05:00 pm | | | | | | | |
| 05:30 pm | | | | | | | |
| 06:00 pm | | | | | | | |
| 06:30 pm | | | | | | | |
| 07:00 pm | | | | | | | |
| 07:30 pm | | | | | | | |
| 08:00 pm | | | | | | | |
| 08:30 pm | | | | | | | |
| 09:00 pm | | | | | | | |
| 09:30 pm | | | | | | | |
| 10:00 pm | | | | | | | |
| 10:30 pm | | | | | | | |

## Important Thoughts / Things to Remember / Doodling

Week Twelve

# Finding Balance: Applying Covey's Last Four Habits to College

## Habit 4: Think Win-Win

In this habit, Covey (2004) challenged his readers to reflect on their relationships and their ability to consider others' needs while also advocating for their own needs in a respectful manner.

Learning to find this balance of courage and consideration leads to win-win outcomes and greater success.

## Activity One: Courage and Consideration

1. In the chart that follows, list all the relationships you have in campus this semester (professors, advisor, Residence Assistant (RA), roommate, classmates, coach, teammates, group/organization leader, work study supervisor and coworkers, etc.). List each of your professors individually.
2. For each relationship, assess whether you lack courage or consideration in that relationship. For example, if you have a C in a course and aren't sure why and are afraid to ask the professor, you are lacking courage to advocate for yourself and do what is necessary to communicate about your grade. However, if you have a C because you have missed many classes, do not participate, and don't turn in assignments, you are lacking consideration in that relationship.
3. Finally, for each relationship, make a goal for restoring balance in that relationship this week by listing one thing you will do to improve in either courage or consideration. For example, if you have been afraid to communicate with the professor, a goal might be to set up an appointment during his or her office hours to discuss your grade. Or, if you need to work on consideration and you consistently arrive late to class, you might make a goal of apologizing to the professor for being late and commit to arriving to class 5 minutes early for the rest of the semester (and keep the commitment!).

| Relationships | Courage or Consideration | Goal for the Week |
|---|---|---|
| | | |
| | | |
| | | |
| | | |
| | | |
| | | |
| | | |
| | | |
| | | |

## Habit 5: Seek First to Understand, Then to Be Understood

While all of Covey's (2004) habits are challenging, I think that this habit is one of the most challenging. We live in a society where we are constantly fed with the message that we should focus on ourselves—take care of ourselves first. Yet, in this habit, we learn to shift the focus to **Other**. This habit gives us the reverse message of society by saying that if we learn to focus on others first, we will find greater success. And, the habit goes even deeper; it teaches us to do something we are terrible at doing. It teaches us to completely shut everything off and listen with all of our senses—and our hearts to another person. This means we need to be quiet. It means we cannot multitask. The phone, computer, and other technological devices need to be put away. We even need to keep our minds from drifting. We need to devote complete and full attention to the other person. This shouldn't be difficult—but it is. Why? Because we seldom do it. Yet, that is what most of us want most desperately—to be listened to by someone else.

Another problem with listening is that when we do make the effort to listen to others, we usually listen from our own frame of reference. This means that we listen on different levels tuning in and out as the information is important to us. Listening with **Other** as a frame of reference forces us to focus on the person who is speaking and that person's needs. This type of listening requires empathic listening where you pay attention to and listen to the other person's body language, tone, expressions, feelings, and words. You listen with your eyes, ears, and heart.

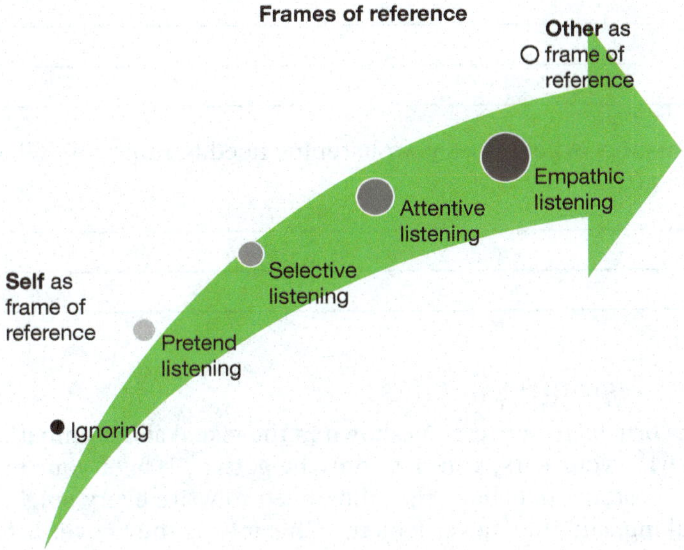


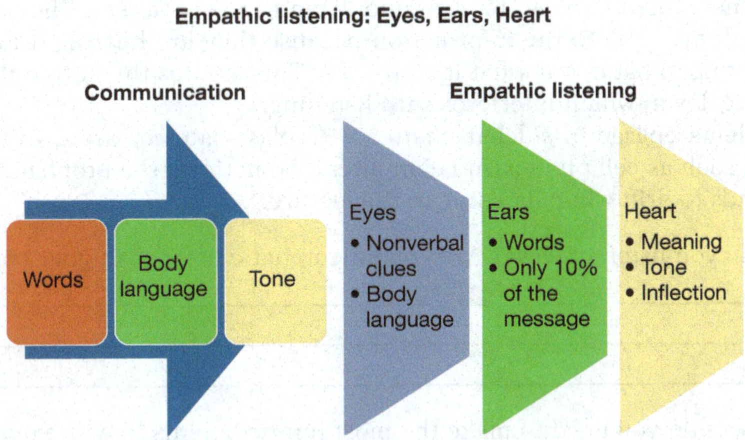

## Activity Two: Empathic Listening

In which of your relationships, do you most struggle with empathic listening? Why?

When have you been completely listened to with full attention? How did this make you feel? What did this person do to make you feel listened to?

In your relationships, where does your listening need to improve? What might you do to be a better listener?

## Activity Three: Listening in Class

Listening in class is crucial to success. As shown in the visual about empathic listening, if you are only listening with your ears, you may only be getting 10% of your professor's message (Covey, 2003). Some students believe that they need to write every single word down while the professor is talking, and they never look up. This means they never listen with their eyes and may miss important body language, expressions and gestures, and the tone of the lecture.

Additionally, many students do not read the textbook before the lecture. Thus, all the information is new when they get to class and listen to the professor. They can't effectively listen and attach meaning to the information because they are hearing it for the first time and are attempting to figure out what it all means. This creates the notion that they should write everything down, which interferes with listening.

Other students engage in sidebar chatter with classmates or are distracted with electronic devices, such as cell phones and computers. Sometimes the problem is that students allow their minds to drift while listening to the lecture.

How well do you listen in class? Are you an emphatic listener in your courses?

Which classes do you need to make the most improvements in with your listening?

What is the problem? What strategy will you implement to improve? What resources are available on campus to help you with this goal?

| Course | Listening Problem | Strategy to Implement | Resources Available on Campus for Support |
|---|---|---|---|
| **E.g., Chemistry** | **Writing everything down and feeling lost during lecture** | **Read before class with SQ3R and create a note-taking template for lecture** | **SWAG sessions (supplemental instruction though the Learning Center)** |
| | | | |
| | | | |
| | | | |
| | | | |
| | | | |
| | | | |

## Habit 6: Synergize

According to Covey (2004), people with synergy might be described as:

- Engaging in creative cooperation and collaboration
- Embracing diversity
- Finding new alternatives
- Stepping and thinking with others outside of the box
- Displaying open mindedness

Where synergy might be most useful for students is the group project. Most students find great struggles and turmoil when working with others on group projects because they don't know how to find synergy. Instead of embracing diversity, they find conflict when diverse opinions and ideas, talents, and personalities emerge. And instead of exploring new alternatives through the diversity, they often try to force one idea on the group. Rather than stepping and thinking with others outside of the box, members try to force others into their narrow boxes of close mindedness. Thus, cooperation and collaboration never occur. Tension rises, and the end result is a project that is less than lack luster—or a project that only reflects one group member's work.

Professors don't assign group projects to torture you! We assign them because we know that the majority of the work you will do outside of college in the workplace will be done in groups and committees. Thus, it is essential that you learn how to work with others. It is essential that you learn how to find synergy.

## Activity Four: Finding Synergy

Reflect on the last group project you worked on—or a group project you are currently working on. What was or is the experience?

What is the greatest difficulty?

How could you help the group find synergy? Be more open to each other's ideas?

Reflect on each group member's unique talents and personality. How might these be challenged to enhance and become a strength for your project? List each group member's name and their unique talents and personality?

How might you help the members recognize their talents and abilities? The group recognize the talents and abilities?

What role can you play in the group to make sure that synergy occurs and that one person does not dominate or shut down ideas? How can you make sure that the group remains open minded and values each member's unique gifts and talents?

______________________________________________

______________________________________________

______________________________________________

______________________________________________

## Habit 7: Sharpen the Saw (Covey, 2004)

The last of the habits encourages us to keep balance in all areas of our life: spiritual, emotional/ social, cognitive, and physical. In order for us to be successful, we need to make sure that we are healthy. Neglecting any of these areas will lead to a deterioration of our well-being and success. Thus, we need to make sure that these areas all are part of our daily routine. We need to carve out time in our planners for each of these areas, or time will never be devoted to them. They need to become one of our big rocks in the jar.

The two most common for students to devote most of their time to are the cognitive and social/emotional. Physical and spiritual are often left off of their planners entirely—unless they are athletes. Then, the physical takes up a good portion of their planners and cognitive may be more difficult to balance.

When talking about spiritual needs, some students may argue that they don't believe in God or don't like to go to church. But, spiritual in its simplest form means being aware of your internal compass. Meeting your spiritual needs means that you are giving some time each day to self-reflection about who you are and where you are headed and why. Some use meditation for this, or Yoga; others use prayer and Scripture, and others spend time in nature.

It is important to remember that with careful planning some of these needs can overlap and be met at the same time. For example, spiritual and physical needs might be met at the same time by going for a walk outside for 30 minutes each day or by praying while walking. Or, you might find a workout buddy and combine social and physical needs. Another idea might be to form a group study and meet both social and cognitive needs at the same time. The main idea is to make sure that you are meeting needs in all the areas!

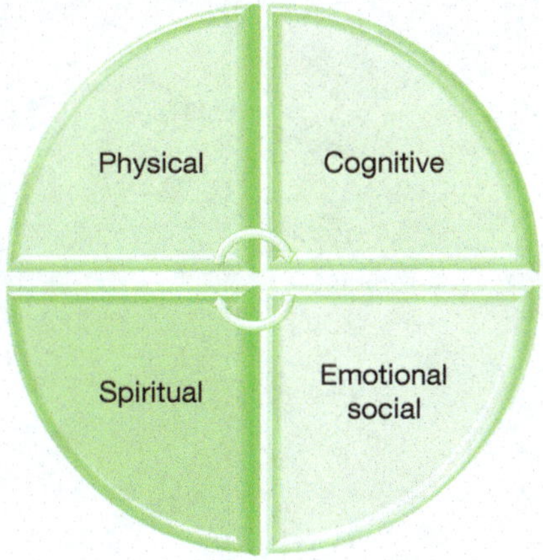

## Activity Five: Spiritual, Physical, Emotional/Social, and Cognitive Needs

Of the four areas (spiritual, physical, emotional/social, and cognitive), in which one do you lack the most balance? What is one goal you will make this week to begin meeting your needs in this area?

______________________________________________________________________________

______________________________________________________________________________

______________________________________________________________________________

______________________________________________________________________________

What resources are available on campus to help you with this goal?

______________________________________________________________________________

______________________________________________________________________________

______________________________________________________________________________

______________________________________________________________________________

## References

Covey, S. R. (2003). *The 7 habits of highly effective people: Personal workbook*. New York: Fire Side.

Covey, S. R. (2004). *The 7 habits of highly effective people: Powerful lessons in personal change.* New York: Free Press.

Every strike brings me closer
to the next home run.

**— Babe Ruth**

## Weekly Goals

**Week of:** ______________________

**What am I grateful for?**

**What are your goal(s) for the week?**

| **Course:** | ________ | ________ | ________ | ________ | ________ | ________ |
|---|---|---|---|---|---|---|
| • To do: | | | | | | |
| • Strateg(ies): | | | | | | |
| • Resource(s): | | | | | | |

**Personal Wellness/Spirituality:**

**Family & Friends:**

**Weekly Planner** **Week of:** ____________________

| | Monday | Tuesday | Wednesday | Thursday | Friday | Saturday | Sunday |
|---|---|---|---|---|---|---|---|
| 06:00 am | | | | | | | |
| 06:30 am | | | | | | | |
| 07:00 am | | | | | | | |
| 07:30 am | | | | | | | |
| 08:00 am | | | | | | | |
| 08:30 am | | | | | | | |
| 09:00 am | | | | | | | |
| 09:30 am | | | | | | | |
| 10:00 am | | | | | | | |
| 10:30 am | | | | | | | |
| 11:00 am | | | | | | | |
| 11:30 am | | | | | | | |
| 12:00 pm | | | | | | | |
| 12:30 pm | | | | | | | |
| 01:00 pm | | | | | | | |
| 01:30 pm | | | | | | | |
| 02:00 pm | | | | | | | |
| 02:30 pm | | | | | | | |
| 03:00 pm | | | | | | | |
| 03:30 pm | | | | | | | |
| 04:00 pm | | | | | | | |
| 04:30 pm | | | | | | | |
| 05:00 pm | | | | | | | |
| 05:30 pm | | | | | | | |
| 06:00 pm | | | | | | | |
| 06:30 pm | | | | | | | |
| 07:00 pm | | | | | | | |
| 07:30 pm | | | | | | | |
| 08:00 pm | | | | | | | |
| 08:30 pm | | | | | | | |
| 09:00 pm | | | | | | | |
| 09:30 pm | | | | | | | |
| 10:00 pm | | | | | | | |
| 10:30 pm | | | | | | | |

## Important Thoughts / Things to Remember / Doodling

## Week Thirteen

# Taking Tests with a Strategic Plan

Students often get so worked up about taking tests that they ONLY see taking a test as the physical act of test taking. What they fail to realize is that most successful test taking begins long before the test. In the way that athletes prepare for games and tournaments, successful students spend time preparing in advance for tests. The past 12 weeks you have been practicing strategies that if implemented on a regular basis will prepare you for your tests and reduce test anxiety.

**Figure 13.1: Strategies for Preparing for Tests**

**Preparing for the test**

- Read before class with active reading strategies such as SQ3R, THIEVES, KWL, or annotating
- Create concept maps and outlines
- Use cornell notes or quiz notes
- Synthesize class notes and book notes
- Quiz yourself with concept cards and self tests on multiple levels of learning using Bloom's Taxonomy
- Use group study

## Activity One: Preparing for the Test

Review Figure 13.1 above and then reflect on how well you have been implementing the strategies by responding to the following questions: How have you been doing on your tests this semester? Which courses do you struggle most with in taking tests?

______________________________________________

How prepared were you for the test? Were your study strategies active? When did you begin studying (at least a week in advance)? How many study sessions did you have? As you review the strategies for preparing for tests, which could you do a better job of implementing in these courses? What changes could you make to your test preparation?

______________________________________________

______________________________________________

### Taking the Test

In addition to preparing for tests in advance, there are some useful test-taking strategies that can increase your academic performance. As with most situations in life, having a strategic plan is helpful. However, many students are so worried about finishing on time that they just immediately get started with the first question. The problem with this approach is that most tests have different point values for different questions. Also, not all question types are of the same level of difficulty. If you begin with the most difficult questions and lose confidence and burn up most of your time on the first page of the test and then realize that the second page of the test is worth the majority of the points—you may not do very well on the test. You may not only find yourself mentally drained, but you might also run out of time and lose a lot points. You might find that you knew the material and were prepared, but your lack of test-taking skills and preparation caused you to get a C rather than an A.

A better approach is to take 5 minutes at the start of the test to quickly scan and read through the entire test and make a plan of attack. Create a time budget where you allow the most amount of time for the questions with the highest amount of points. Also, begin with the easiest questions first. This will allow you to build confidence and momentum. Skip questions you do not know (but mark them), and return to them later. This keeps you from wasting time and becoming unnecessarily anxious over one question that might only be worth a few points.

Also, as you read questions, underline key words so that you don't miss important words or misinterpret questions. As you answer the questions, look back at the words you underlined and make sure your answer fits with the key words you are being assessed over.

## Figure 13.2: Test-taking Strategies

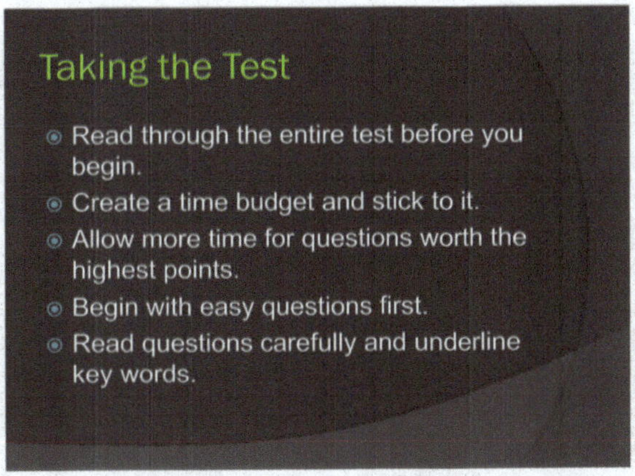


## Multiple Choice Questions

Students either love multiple choice questions or they hate them. Personally, I always hated them. I was one of those students who tended to overanalyze multiple choice questions. I preferred essay exams! Needless to say, I was a literature major.

If you are one of the students (as I was) who overthinks and struggles with multiple choice questions, you might find the following strategies helpful.

## Figure 13.3: Strategies for Multiple Choice Exams

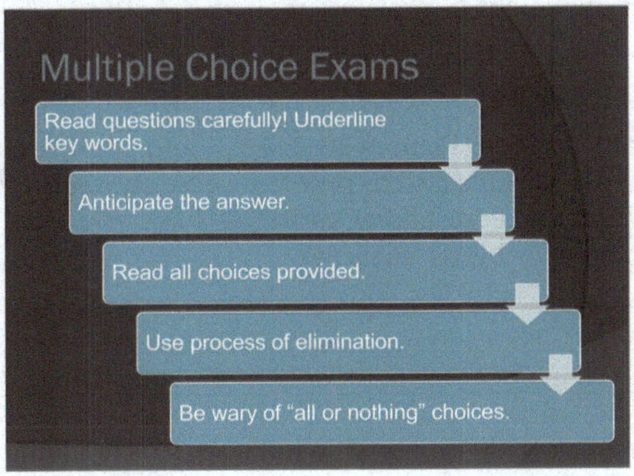


## True/False Questions

True/False questions are also easy to overthink. Those of us who tend to overanalyze tend to struggle with these questions also. It is helpful to remember that most true/false questions are simple knowledge-level questions. They are simply checks of information at the lowest level. They are not intended to trick you! So, don't overanalyze them. You should also know

**Figure 13.4: Strategies for True/False Questions**

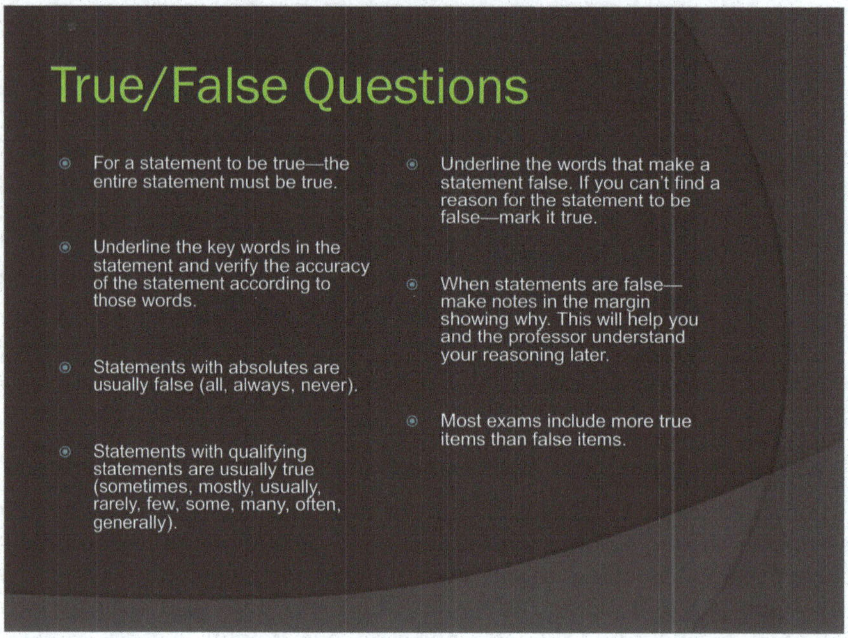


that research tells us that when students change their answers—they tend to change them to an incorrect answer. Avoid the temptation to change your answer unless you absolutely know for sure (without any doubt) that you made a mistake on the first answer. The following tips for true/false questions might improve your success with true/false questions.

## Activity Two: Test Taking

After review and reflecting on Figures 13.2, 13.3, and 13.4, use the following questions to assess your test-taking skills and to problem solve strategies that might help you find greater success. Which of these taking strategies have you tried? What was the result? How might you adapt it for better success?

______________________________________________

______________________________________________

______________________________________________

What is your greatest struggle on tests? What new strategies did you find here that you will implement in the future to find greater success? How might they solve some of your problems?

______________________________________________

______________________________________________

______________________________________________

______________________________________________

## Essay Questions

Most students who prefer objective style tests with multiple choice and true/false questions do not like essay exams. And, those of us who struggled with overanalyzing multiple choice and true/false test questions found great success on the essay exam tests. Regardless of which group you are in, there are definite strategies that make for success on essay exams. Not surprisingly, success with essay exams begins with a plan! Students who just read the essay question and begin writing tend to get low scores on essay exams. Students who find success on essay exams tend to utilize the following strategies.

## Essay Exam Tips

- **Directions.** Read directions carefully. Pay attention to the details. Underline key words if needed. (Do you need to respond to all questions? Are all questions worth the same amount of points?)
- **Strategize.** Pay attention to the time and strategize. How much time do you have? Create a time budget that allows: outlining/pre-writing, responding to the questions, proofreading. Allow more time for the questions with the higher point values and begin with those questions first. Hold yourself to your time budget.
- **Direction words.** Underline the important direction words and craft your response in accordance with the words.

**Figure 13.5: Common Direction Words used in Essay Exams**

| Direction word | Meaning |
|---|---|
| Compare | Give similarities |
| Contrast | Give differences |
| Compare and contrast | Give similarities and differences |
| Define | Give the meaning with limited detail |
| Support | Give specific examples that back up what you are saying |
| Explain | Offer examples |
| Describe | Give meaning with lots of detail |
| Discuss | Give brief background/meaning surrounding the topic that shows you have understanding and offer reasons (pro and con) with supporting details |

| Direction word | Meaning |
|---|---|
| Evaluate | Offer your judgment and support with examples |
| Illustrate | Give an example |
| Justify | Give reasons |
| Cause/effect | Give steps leading to a situation or event |
| Relate | Show how ideas and concepts connect |

## Five-Paragraph Structure

While the five-paragraph structure does not work well for most class writing assignments, it is very effective for essay exams that require more than a short response. Use this structure if the exam is expecting a detailed and developed response of one page or more.

### Introduction

Rephrase the question into a thesis statement. Use the same words from the question and then add what you will specifically address in your response. Move from general to specific. If your response requires support, offer three examples in the thesis that you will use for support.

> ***Example***
>
> Question: Discuss a need for students to use an Academic Learning Center while they are attending college.
>
> Introduction/Thesis Statement:
> College students often struggle with transitioning from high school to college. By **using an Academic Learning Center while they are attending college, students** learn how to effectively manage their time, read critically and efficiently, and apply test-taking and study strategies.

### Response

Stick to your thesis statement. Do not bring in any new information. Devote one paragraph to each example listed in your thesis. So, your response should have **three paragraphs**.

> Example of paragraph one about time management (first example in thesis).
>
> Surveys show that most high school students spend 2–3 hours per week studying. College professors expect students to spend 2–3 hours studying outside of class for each credit hour they are enrolled in. This means that students enrolled in 15 credit hours need to be studying outside of class 30–45 hours a week. Thus, college equates with a full-time job. The difference between high school and college expectations for studying and academic work often overwhelms students. The Academic Learning Center helps students feel less overwhelmed by helping them apply time management strategies that will allow students to devote an adequate amount of time to studying while also allowing time for recreation.

## Conclusion

Briefly summarize and bring everything together in one to two sentences. Then, provide a "so what." Explain why it is relevant and important to consider the topic or issue. Apply it to current events or your own situation. The "so what" component is often what separates A essay responses from B essay responses.

> Example of a "so what" conclusion:
> Given the struggles previously discussed that new college students often have with time management, college level reading, and test performance, the Academic Learning Center clearly becomes one of the most important resources on a college campus. College administrators are also becoming more aware of this resource, as academic probation becomes a threat to retention and the Board of Regents demands higher graduation rates from state universities.

**Figure 13.6: Outline of 5-Paragraph Essay Response**

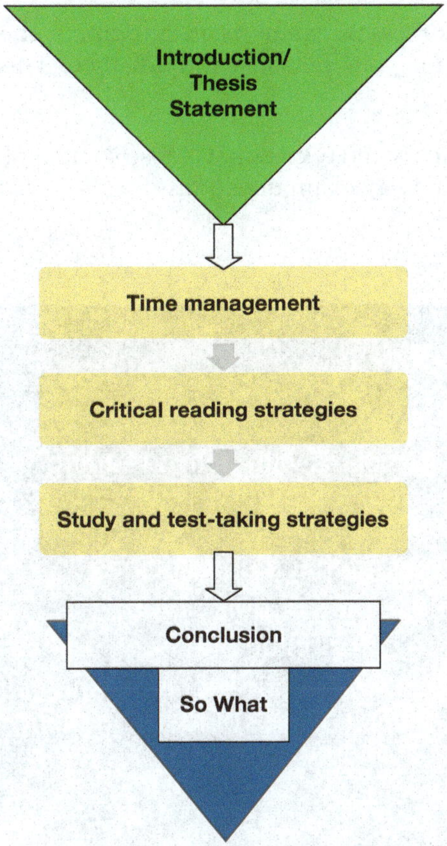

## Activity Three: Essay Exams

After reviewing and reflecting on the suggested essay exam strategies, use the following questions to assess which of these strategies you might help you find greater success on essay exams. How have you performed on essay exams in the past?

______________________________________________________________________

What methods have you used? Based on this new information presented, what new methods might you try?

______________________________________________________________________

______________________________________________________________________

## Activity Four: Anticipating Essay Exams

In which courses are you most likely to face essay exams?

______________________________________________________________________

______________________________________________________________________

The best way to prepare for essay exams is to anticipate the questions you might face and then prepare outlines for your responses in advance. This is also an excellent study strategy!

1. Look through your notes and textbook. Choose some topics that your professor might decide to assess with essay exam questions.

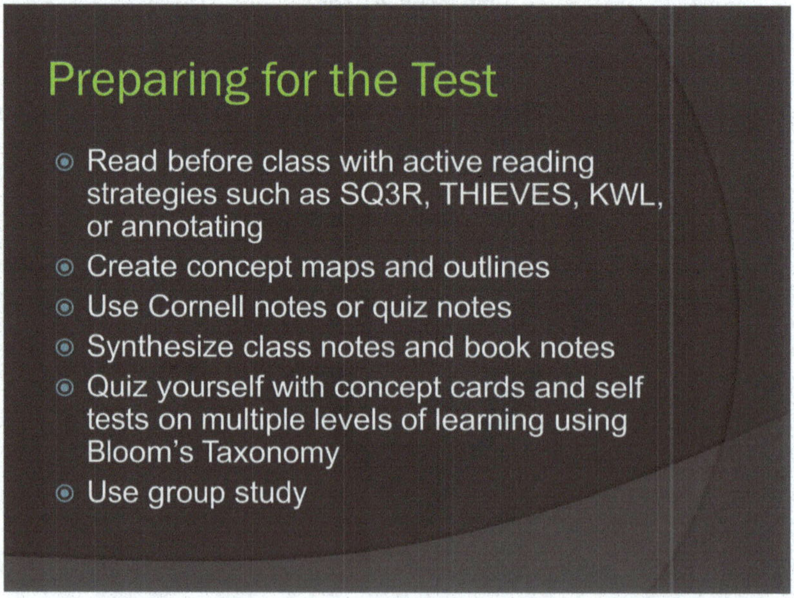

2. Use the word chart (Figure 13.5) that appears earlier in this section to write some essay exam questions. Imagine you are your professor. How does he or she write questions? What were they like in the past? Write the questions in his or her style. (Better yet, do this as a group study. Have each group member anticipate and write an essay question!) Essay exam questions are usually higher on Bloom's Taxonomy. So, your questions should be application, evaluation, analysis, synthesis, or evaluation questions.
3. Write a thesis and outline for responding to the question. Don't look at your notes or textbook. See what you know on your own. (If you are doing this as a group, exchange questions.)
4. Use your notes and textbook to check your response. (If you are working with a group, correct each other's responses.)

## Activity Five: Planning to Write a Paper

This organization structure can also be used with writing papers. In place of the example paragraphs—plan for pages. For instance, example one could be 1–2 pages of support of the example or first point of the thesis, example two might be 1–2 pages, and example three could be 1–2 pages. Follow the same formats for the introduction and conclusion, as suggested for the essay exam.

Mapping out a paper in this way helps you to build a structure and timeline. Then, each 1–2-page section becomes like a mini essay that could be worked on in a 2-3 hour study session on your study schedule. Following this method, you can map out the writing of the paper over days (a week) and reduce anxiety and procrastination in writing a paper. For example:

- Day One: Introduction and Thesis/half page
- Day Two: First Point of Thesis/1–2 pages
- Day Three: Second Point of Thesis/1–2 pages
- Day Four: Third Point of Thesis/1–2 pages
- Day Five: Conclusion and revise introduction based on what paper reflects
- Day Six: Meet with Writing Center for suggested revisions and feedback
- Day Seven: Revise paper based on feedback; proofread grammar, polish word choice, combine and strengthen sentences

*Research, thinking, and active reading will also need to be built into the paper before the writing even begins.

1. Read the assignment guidelines for one of your papers that you need to write this semester.
2. Use the writing a paper concept map to organize a plan for your paper.
    - Write your thesis in the Introduction triangle, include three main points that you will argue or discuss and that fits the assignment and your research (if required). This will be the last sentence of your introduction.

- ❖ In the first box, write the first main point of your thesis and support you will use to back up this point. Note counter claims to address.
- ❖ In the second box, write the second main point of your thesis and support you will use to back up this point. Note counter claims to address.
- ❖ In the third box, write the third main point of your thesis and support you will use to back up this point. Note counter claims to address.
- ❖ In the conclusion triangle, write some summary points of your paper and ideas for the so what. Why is it important and relevant.

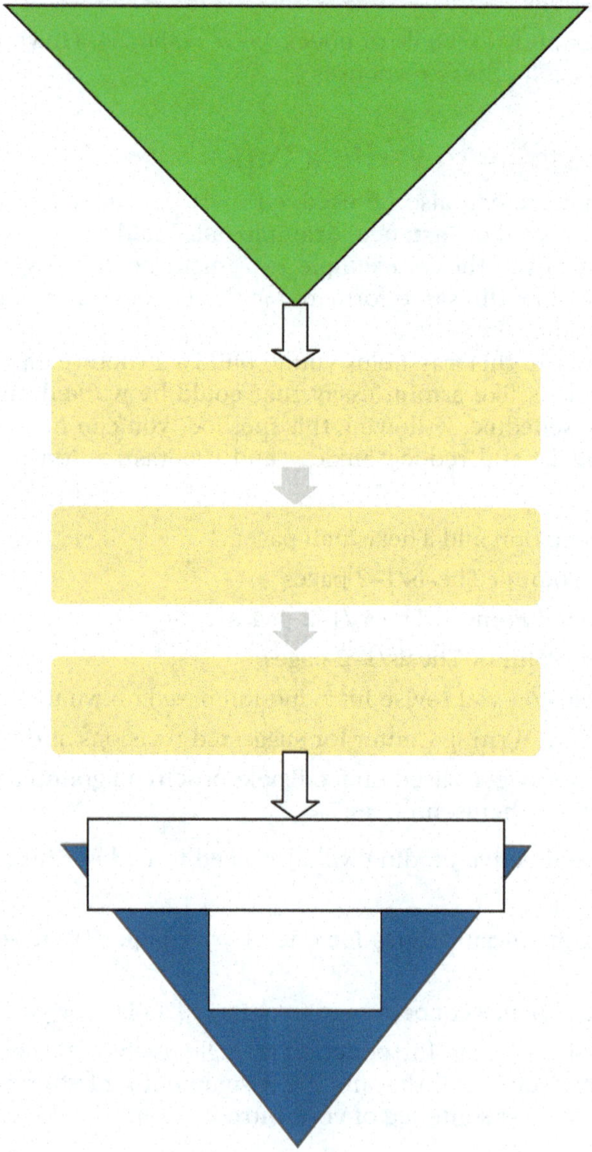

3. Using your study schedule—include days/times you will devote to each section of the paper. Use the example timeline in this activity for a guide:

❖ Day One: Introduction and Thesis/half page
**Day/Time:**

❖ Day Two: First Point of Thesis/1–2 pages
**Day/Time:**

❖ Day Three: Second Point of Thesis/1–2 pages
**Day/Time:**

❖ Day Four: Third Point of Thesis/1–2 pages
**Day/Time:**

❖ Day Five: Conclusion and revise introduction based on what paper reflects
**Day/Time:**

❖ Day Six: Meet with Writing Center for suggested revisions and feedback
**Appointment time:**

❖ Day Seven: Revise paper based on feedback; proofread grammar, polish word choice, combine and strengthen sentences
**Day/Time:**

**Weekly Goals** **Week of:** ____________________

| **What am I grateful for?**<br><br>**What are your goal(s) for the week?** | | | | | | |
|---|---|---|---|---|---|---|
| **Course:** | ________ | ________ | ________ | ________ | ________ | ________ |
| • To do: | | | | | | |
| • Strateg(ies): | | | | | | |
| • Resource(s): | | | | | | |

| | |
|---|---|
| **Personal Wellness/Spirituality:** | 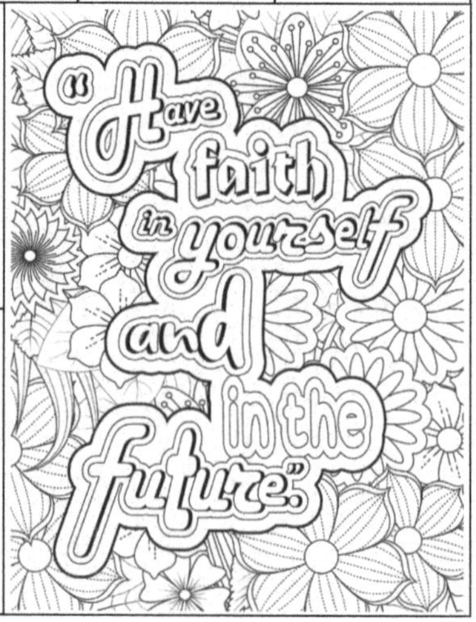 |
| **Family & Friends:** | |

**Weekly Planner** **Week of:** ____________________

| | Monday | Tuesday | Wednesday | Thursday | Friday | Saturday | Sunday |
|---|---|---|---|---|---|---|---|
| 06:00 am | | | | | | | |
| 06:30 am | | | | | | | |
| 07:00 am | | | | | | | |
| 07:30 am | | | | | | | |
| 08:00 am | | | | | | | |
| 08:30 am | | | | | | | |
| 09:00 am | | | | | | | |
| 09:30 am | | | | | | | |
| 10:00 am | | | | | | | |
| 10:30 am | | | | | | | |
| 11:00 am | | | | | | | |
| 11:30 am | | | | | | | |
| 12:00 pm | | | | | | | |
| 12:30 pm | | | | | | | |
| 01:00 pm | | | | | | | |
| 01:30 pm | | | | | | | |
| 02:00 pm | | | | | | | |
| 02:30 pm | | | | | | | |
| 03:00 pm | | | | | | | |
| 03:30 pm | | | | | | | |
| 04:00 pm | | | | | | | |
| 04:30 pm | | | | | | | |
| 05:00 pm | | | | | | | |
| 05:30 pm | | | | | | | |
| 06:00 pm | | | | | | | |
| 06:30 pm | | | | | | | |
| 07:00 pm | | | | | | | |
| 07:30 pm | | | | | | | |
| 08:00 pm | | | | | | | |
| 08:30 pm | | | | | | | |
| 09:00 pm | | | | | | | |
| 09:30 pm | | | | | | | |
| 10:00 pm | | | | | | | |
| 10:30 pm | | | | | | | |

## Important Thoughts / Things to Remember / Doodling

Week Fourteen

# Overcoming Test Anxiety

One of the most common complaints I hear from students is that they have test anxiety. They freeze up during the test and can't think straight. They study but can't show their true ability because they get nervous, and anxiety interferes with their performance.

Anxiety is real. It isn't just an excuse made up to avoid facing failure. It really does occur and affect performance. Many students deal with test anxiety. Some students actually discover that their anxiety is more serious than test anxiety and is a medical condition that requires treatment beyond what this chapter will suggest. (If you find that anxiety has impacted more areas of your life than exams, and it has been going on for a long time, you should schedule an appointment with your medical provider to see if you are dealing with more than test anxiety.)

Test anxiety is your body's physical reaction to stress, and it can manifest in many different physical symptoms: headache, nausea, rapid heart rate, vomiting, confusion, mind going blank, diarrhea, fainting, unavoidable crying, shaking, feeling tense, sweaty palms, and so on. Once your body begins to react in this manner, your cognitive function is impaired and your performance is negatively affected. So, how do you combat test anxiety? Below are some of the most commonly suggested tips by professionals.

- **Prepare** for the test well in advance! Do not cram the night before a test. Regular reviewing and studying of material should occur throughout the semester. (The Academic Learning Center staff on your campus can help you develop strategies for this!) You will feel more confident if the material is in your long-term memory rather than short-term memory. Remember that **studying is practicing to take the test**!
- **Exercise** regularly, and then get plenty of sleep the night before the test. Staying up all night *reduces* your chances for a good grade.
- **Eat** well-balanced and healthy meals—but don't overeat. Keep your energy level high with small and light snacks, such as nuts, cheese, and fruit (especially citrus) throughout studying and before the test. If you are permitted to take food and drink into the classroom, take something with you to keep your energy high, especially if it's a long exam. Water is a good choice, but too much caffeine might create anxiety.

- **Plan ahead** so that you arrive **on time** at the testing site with pencils, pens, and paper (whatever you'll need)! Wearing a watch is always a good idea. Some rooms do not have visible clocks, and you will be required to put your cell phone out of sight.
- **Arrive early (but not too early)**, and do *not* pull out notes and cram right before the exam. Instead, relax and breathe deeply. Put your hand on your stomach right below your rib cage. Feel it move in and out while you slowly inhale and exhale. Consciously release tension throughout your body—from your head to your toes.
- **Free write** about your test anxieties 10 minutes before taking the exam. A recent University of Chicago Study shows that this allows you to release your worries before the exam begins so that you can remember what you have learned and studied (http://news.uchicago.edu/article/2011/01/13/writing-about-worries-eases-anxiety-and-improves-test-performance).
- **Begin with the easiest questions first and be confident**. This is your chance to find out what ideas your instructor thinks are important, and it's also your opportunity to show what you know.
- **Read carefully** all directions and questions. Underline key words.
- **Budget your** time before you begin. Note the number of questions and the point values. On scratch paper or in the margin of the test, create a time plan for the total allotted time of the testing period. Begin with and assign the most amount of time to the questions with the highest point value. Allow for time to proofread and review your responses.
- **Pace yourself and do not panic** if you are not the first one done. You will be graded on your answers, not your speed. If you finish early, make sure you responded to all the questions and followed directions. But—don't change your answers.

## Activity One: Reflecting on Test Anxiety

When was the last time that you became nervous and anxious while taking a test? At what point during the test did you become anxious? What do you think triggered it?

______________________________________________

______________________________________________

______________________________________________

How has test anxiety affected your performance in the past? Which subjects is it most related to?

______________________________________________

______________________________________________

______________________________________________

Looking back at your reflection and the suggestions for avoiding test anxiety, what are some steps you could take to combat test anxiety in the future?

______________________________________________

______________________________________________

______________________________________________

## Activity Two: Campus Connections for Combatting Test Anxiety

1. What campus resources are available to help you take the steps needed to combat your test anxiety? Use the list below to identify some resources that might help in making the next steps.
   - ❖ Better preparation—learning center or writing center
   - ❖ Coping/relaxation/stress reduction—counseling center
   - ❖ Better study techniques—learning center
   - ❖ Time management—learning center
   - ❖ Identifying learning disabilities and receiving accommodations—disability services
   - ❖ Test-taking strategies—learning center
2. Look back at the campus resource chart from Week One and find the contact information for these resources.
3. Call and set up an appointment to meet with the resource people to implement your steps in reducing test anxiety!

**Weekly Goals** **Week of:** ____________________

**What am I grateful for?**

**What are your goal(s) for the week?**

| **Course:** | ______ | ______ | ______ | ______ | ______ | ______ |
|---|---|---|---|---|---|---|
| • To do: | | | | | | |
| • Strateg(ies): | | | | | | |
| • Resource(s): | | | | | | |

**Personal Wellness/Spirituality:**

**Family & Friends:**

**Weekly Planner** **Week of:** ______________________

| | Monday | Tuesday | Wednesday | Thursday | Friday | Saturday | Sunday |
|---|---|---|---|---|---|---|---|
| 06:00 am | | | | | | | |
| 06:30 am | | | | | | | |
| 07:00 am | | | | | | | |
| 07:30 am | | | | | | | |
| 08:00 am | | | | | | | |
| 08:30 am | | | | | | | |
| 09:00 am | | | | | | | |
| 09:30 am | | | | | | | |
| 10:00 am | | | | | | | |
| 10:30 am | | | | | | | |
| 11:00 am | | | | | | | |
| 11:30 am | | | | | | | |
| 12:00 pm | | | | | | | |
| 12:30 pm | | | | | | | |
| 01:00 pm | | | | | | | |
| 01:30 pm | | | | | | | |
| 02:00 pm | | | | | | | |
| 02:30 pm | | | | | | | |
| 03:00 pm | | | | | | | |
| 03:30 pm | | | | | | | |
| 04:00 pm | | | | | | | |
| 04:30 pm | | | | | | | |
| 05:00 pm | | | | | | | |
| 05:30 pm | | | | | | | |
| 06:00 pm | | | | | | | |
| 06:30 pm | | | | | | | |
| 07:00 pm | | | | | | | |
| 07:30 pm | | | | | | | |
| 08:00 pm | | | | | | | |
| 08:30 pm | | | | | | | |
| 09:00 pm | | | | | | | |
| 09:30 pm | | | | | | | |
| 10:00 pm | | | | | | | |
| 10:30 pm | | | | | | | |

## Important Thoughts / Things to Remember / Doodling

Week Fifteen

# Preparing for Finals

You have worked hard all semester, and you want to finish strong. Finals can either help your grade or hinder your grade. One thing is certain—the commonly described all-night cram session before a college final fueled with a pot of coffee is not the most effective method for succeeding on your final exam. Actually, it is likely to leave you jittery, tired, and with information that has not been stored in your long-term memory.

The best way to prepare is to continue using the strategies you have learned throughout these past few weeks. Stick to your study schedule, use active study strategies, manage your time and stress, and apply the test-taking strategies from last week.

However, there are a few other helpful strategies that might make you more prepared for the final. The activities included this week will help you prepare in advance for finals week.

## Activity One: Finals Week Schedule

Finals week tends to always present a few challenges with scheduling because the test schedule is often different from your regular schedule. Unfortunately, this schedule is not always communicated in an obvious place or by professors weeks in advance. First-year students are often thrown off when they find out at the last minute that finals week is different than their normal schedule.

To find the schedule for finals week, go to the Registrar's or academic affairs' page on the college website. Look for Academic Calendars and then search for Finals Schedule and the year of the semester. There, you will find the schedule for finals. Look for the times that your class normally meets and to find the time for the final. Use the chart below to create a schedule for your finals. Then, write your finals in your planner.

| Course | Day/time | Room |
|---|---|---|
| | | |
| | | |
| | | |
| | | |
| | | |
| | | |

## Activity Two: Studying for Finals—5-Day Study Plan

Using the 5-day study plan is an effective method for studying for finals that allows you to review multiple chapters before a cumulative exam without cramming. It also allows you to study for multiple courses at the same time. The key is careful mapping and planning in advance and implementation of the strategies you have been using and practicing all semester.

The way it works is that on day one you begin reviewing the first chapter in the sequence with active study strategies. On day two, you review that same chapter again for half of the study block and then add the next chapter in the sequence to the second half of your study block and review that chapter with active study strategies. On day three, you spend about ¼ of the time reviewing the first chapter and divide the remaining time of the study block and use it for reviewing the second and third chapters. And, you continue in this manner for all 5 days before your finals for each of your courses. This allows you to effectively review all the material repetitively in looping study manner.

**Figure 15.1: Sample 5-day Study Plan**

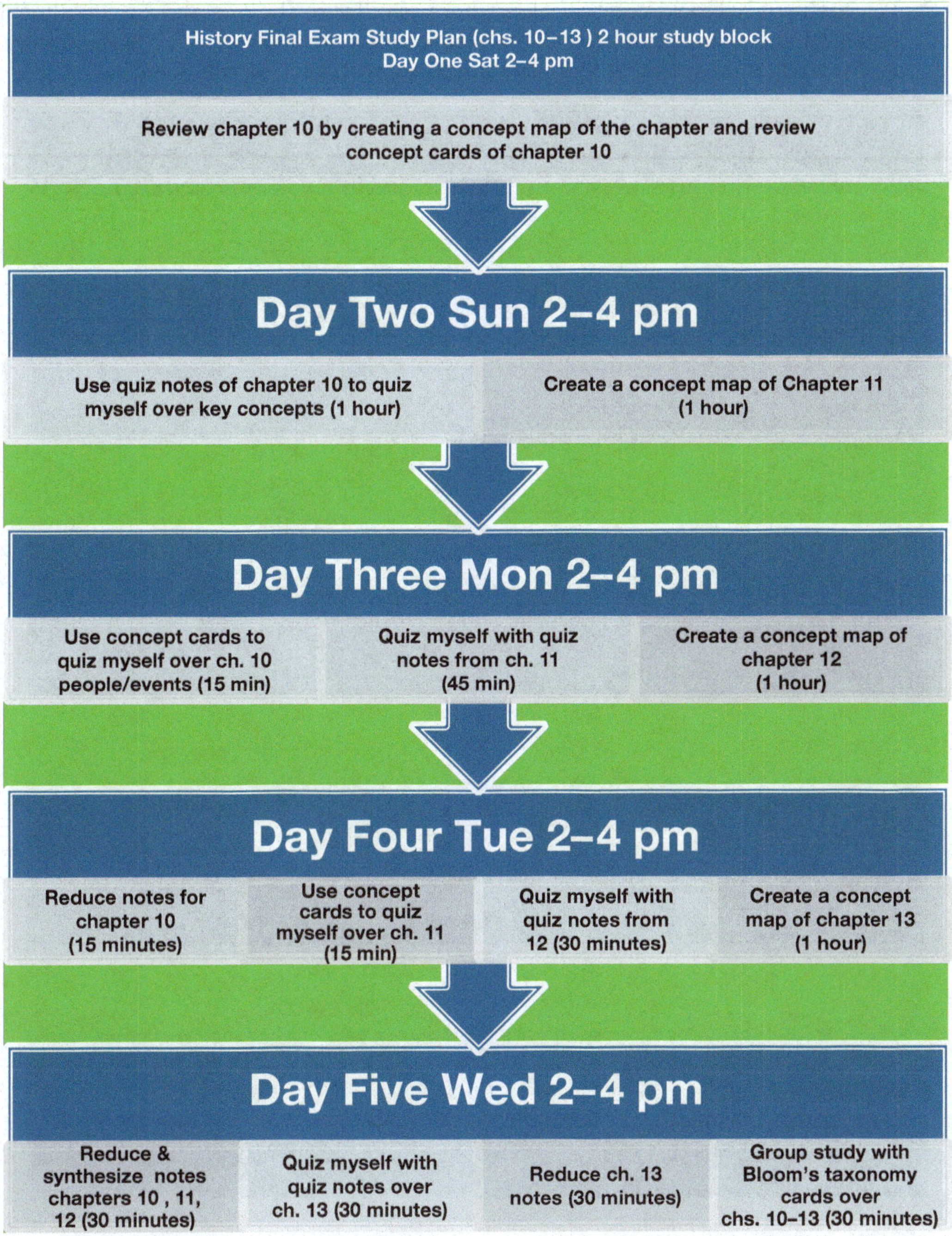

1. Map out a study schedule in which you carve out five study blocks (1–2 hours for each block) for each of your finals.
2. For each study block, create a plan where (similar to the one above) you allow for repeated and incremental review of each chapter throughout the 5 days using the active study strategies that you have practiced with success this semester.

If there is no struggle,
there is no progress.

**— Frederick Douglass**

**Weekly Goals** **Week of:** ____________________

**What am I grateful for?**

**What are your goal(s) for the week?**

| Course: | | | | | | |
|---|---|---|---|---|---|---|
| • To do: | | | | | | |
| • Strateg(ies): | | | | | | |
| • Resource(s): | | | | | | |

**Personal Wellness/Spirituality:**

**Family & Friends:**

**Weekly Planner** **Week of:** ______________________

| | Monday | Tuesday | Wednesday | Thursday | Friday | Saturday | Sunday |
|---|---|---|---|---|---|---|---|
| 06:00 am | | | | | | | |
| 06:30 am | | | | | | | |
| 07:00 am | | | | | | | |
| 07:30 am | | | | | | | |
| 08:00 am | | | | | | | |
| 08:30 am | | | | | | | |
| 09:00 am | | | | | | | |
| 09:30 am | | | | | | | |
| 10:00 am | | | | | | | |
| 10:30 am | | | | | | | |
| 11:00 am | | | | | | | |
| 11:30 am | | | | | | | |
| 12:00 pm | | | | | | | |
| 12:30 pm | | | | | | | |
| 01:00 pm | | | | | | | |
| 01:30 pm | | | | | | | |
| 02:00 pm | | | | | | | |
| 02:30 pm | | | | | | | |
| 03:00 pm | | | | | | | |
| 03:30 pm | | | | | | | |
| 04:00 pm | | | | | | | |
| 04:30 pm | | | | | | | |
| 05:00 pm | | | | | | | |
| 05:30 pm | | | | | | | |
| 06:00 pm | | | | | | | |
| 06:30 pm | | | | | | | |
| 07:00 pm | | | | | | | |
| 07:30 pm | | | | | | | |
| 08:00 pm | | | | | | | |
| 08:30 pm | | | | | | | |
| 09:00 pm | | | | | | | |
| 09:30 pm | | | | | | | |
| 10:00 pm | | | | | | | |
| 10:30 pm | | | | | | | |

## Important Thoughts / Things to Remember / Doodling

# Week Sixteen

# Review, Assess, and Reflect

Congratulations! You have made it to the last week of the semester. Now, that you are here, it is good while everything is still fresh in your memory to think back over the semester and reflect on the new strategies you have tried and the progress you have made. It is also helpful to reflect on how you will continue that growth next semester and begin to make those goals now. This week's activities will help facilitate that process.

## Activity One: Self-Assessment

1. At the beginning of the semester, you assessed yourself on the key skill areas that affect academic success. Use that same self-assessment to evaluate yourself in those areas again.

## Figure 16.1: Self-Assessment

**Date:**

(5 is highest)

1. How are you feeling about your skills in the following areas:

| | | | | | |
|---|---|---|---|---|---|
| Reading | 1 | 2 | 3 | 4 | 5 |
| Writing | 1 | 2 | 3 | 4 | 5 |
| Note-Taking | 1 | 2 | 3 | 4 | 5 |
| Time Management | 1 | 2 | 3 | 4 | 5 |
| Organization | 1 | 2 | 3 | 4 | 5 |
| Test-Taking | 1 | 2 | 3 | 4 | 5 |
| Oral Communication | 1 | 2 | 3 | 4 | 5 |
| Studying | 1 | 2 | 3 | 4 | 5 |
| Motivation | 1 | 2 | 3 | 4 | 5 |

For those that are not "5," what do you feel would help you get to a "5"?

Which skill areas have most impacted your success in the past?

How can this course help?

2. How do you feel about taking this course? Why?

3. What strategies will you use in this course to be successful?

4. What technology needs do you have? How might you address these needs? What gaps may still exist?

5. What challenges do you have this semester that might impact your success in this course that your professor should be aware of? How do you plan to meet these challenges? (Make a plan for communicating needs with professor).

6. What resources will you use to be successful in this course (Ex. Writing Center, Learning Center, Counseling Center, Library, Campus Ministry, IT, Compass/Career Center)?

7. What goals do you wish to make for this semester? What support do you need to achieve these goals?

2. Look back at your self-assessment from week one of the semester.
3. Reflect on and respond to the following questions:

In what areas have you improved?

______________________________________________________________________

______________________________________________________________________

______________________________________________________________________

In what areas do you still need to work on improving?

______________________________________________________________________

______________________________________________________________________

______________________________________________________________________

What resources are available on campus that you could use to help you improve in those areas?

______________________________________________________________________

______________________________________________________________________

______________________________________________________________________

What changes could you implement next semester to improve in those areas?

______________________________________________________________________

______________________________________________________________________

______________________________________________________________________

Thinking ahead of the courses you are registered for next semester, what new strategies and habits that you have implemented will be most important for you to continue using and develop further?

______________________________________________________________________

______________________________________________________________________

______________________________________________________________________

## Activity Two: Goal Setting for Next Semester

1. During week one, you also identified strengths and weaknesses in each of the important academic skill areas to set goals for the semester. In looking ahead to next semester, complete the goal setting chart again.

## Figure 16.2: Goal Setting

Most Students find success when they make adjustments in the following areas. Use the chart to evaluate yourself in these areas and set some goals. **Example of a specific goal that could be demonstrated and assessed: Time Management: I will create a "to do" list each Sunday and write what I need to get done on my planner for the week.**

**Goal that is too general: Use my time effectively.**

| | | |
|---|---|---|
| **Reading**<br><br>**SMI INFP** | **Strengths:**<br><br>**Weaknesses:** | **Goals** |
| **Organization**<br><br>**MOT ANX TMT ATT** | **Strengths:**<br><br>**Weaknesses:** | **Goals** |
| **Studying**<br><br>**SFT UAR** | **Strengths:**<br><br>**Weaknesses:** | **Goals** |
| **Test-Taking**<br><br>**TST UAR** | **Strengths:**<br><br>**Weaknesses:** | **Goals** |
| **Time Management**<br><br>**TST UAR** | **Strengths:**<br><br>**Weaknesses:** | **Goals** |
| **Oral Communication**<br><br>**INFP SMI ANX ATT UAR** | **Strengths:**<br><br>**Weaknesses:** | **Goals** |
| **Motivation/Growth Mindset**<br><br>**MOT ANX ATT** | **Strengths:**<br><br>**Weaknesses:** | **Goals** |

2. In which areas of the LASSI did you see the most growth? What changes resulted in that growth?

3. Which areas of the LASSI still need improvement? What will you do to work on these areas and continue your growth?

4. Look back over your goal sheet from week one and compare it the goal sheet you just completed.
5. As you compare and contrast the two charts, respond to the following questions to reflect on your progress and how you can continue to grow and progress next semester.
   - What new strengths have you acquired since week one?

     ______________________________

     ______________________________

     ______________________________

   - Which goals did you achieve? And, how did you achieve them?

     ______________________________

     ______________________________

     ______________________________

   - What new goals have you set? What steps will you take to achieve the goals?

     ______________________________

     ______________________________

     ______________________________

   - In reflecting on the goals you have set, what are the biggest challenges that you foresee that you will need to overcome next semester?

     ______________________________

     ______________________________

     ______________________________

   - What strategies will you implement to address and overcome these challenges? What resources could you use for support?

     ______________________________

     ______________________________

     ______________________________

❖ What goals from last semester, have carried over for next semester? How will you continue to work on those goals?

______________________________________________

______________________________________________

______________________________________________

❖ In looking at and reflecting on your growth over the semester, which achievements are you most proud of? Why?

______________________________________________

______________________________________________

______________________________________________

## Weekly Goals

**Week of:** ______________________

**What am I grateful for?**

**What are your goal(s) for the week?**

| **Course:** | ________ | ________ | ________ | ________ | ________ | ________ |
|---|---|---|---|---|---|---|
| • To do: | | | | | | |
| • Strateg(ies): | | | | | | |
| • Resource(s): | | | | | | |

**Personal Wellness/Spirituality:**

**Family & Friends:**

**Weekly Planner** **Week of:** ____________________

| | Monday | Tuesday | Wednesday | Thursday | Friday | Saturday | Sunday |
|---|---|---|---|---|---|---|---|
| 06:00 am | | | | | | | |
| 06:30 am | | | | | | | |
| 07:00 am | | | | | | | |
| 07:30 am | | | | | | | |
| 08:00 am | | | | | | | |
| 08:30 am | | | | | | | |
| 09:00 am | | | | | | | |
| 09:30 am | | | | | | | |
| 10:00 am | | | | | | | |
| 10:30 am | | | | | | | |
| 11:00 am | | | | | | | |
| 11:30 am | | | | | | | |
| 12:00 pm | | | | | | | |
| 12:30 pm | | | | | | | |
| 01:00 pm | | | | | | | |
| 01:30 pm | | | | | | | |
| 02:00 pm | | | | | | | |
| 02:30 pm | | | | | | | |
| 03:00 pm | | | | | | | |
| 03:30 pm | | | | | | | |
| 04:00 pm | | | | | | | |
| 04:30 pm | | | | | | | |
| 05:00 pm | | | | | | | |
| 05:30 pm | | | | | | | |
| 06:00 pm | | | | | | | |
| 06:30 pm | | | | | | | |
| 07:00 pm | | | | | | | |
| 07:30 pm | | | | | | | |
| 08:00 pm | | | | | | | |
| 08:30 pm | | | | | | | |
| 09:00 pm | | | | | | | |
| 09:30 pm | | | | | | | |
| 10:00 pm | | | | | | | |
| 10:30 pm | | | | | | | |

## Important Thoughts / Things to Remember / Doodling